The Cheese (

THE *CHEESE* COOKBOOK

Recipes for Every Occasion

PAM CARY

The Crowood Press

First published in 1989 by
The Crowood Press
Ramsbury, Marlborough
Wiltshire SN8 2HE

British Library Cataloguing in Publication Data
Cary, Pam
The cheese cookbook.
1. Food. Cheese dishes. Recipes
I. Title
641.6'73

ISBN 1 85223 163 7

Typeset by Avonset, Midsomer Norton, Nr. Bath
Printed and bound in Great Britain by Biddles Ltd, Guildford & Kings Lynn

Contents

Preface

In writing this book, and therefore broadening my own appreciation for cheese ten-fold, I have come to two main conclusions: one, that the versatility of cheese is limitless, and two, how very lucky those people are who are living in Great Britain. I will stand up and say that I truly believe that on this small island are produced some of the best, most delicious and certainly the most varied cheeses to be found anywhere. The brilliance of British cheese is acknowledged the world over, and, thanks to efficient transportation and exportation, the world is fortunate enough to be able to share this tradition with the British.

The British are not only lucky living with their own cheeses, but have the good fortune to be on the doorstep of Europe, which also enjoys a huge variety of cheeses to suit every taste and desire. Anyone can walk into their local supermarket today and be stuck for choice. Never before has such a huge selection of cheeses been at our fingertips, from France, Italy, Holland, Greece, Switzerland . . . the list is endless.

Cheese selection and tasting is an art that I have come to appreciate during the writing of this book, and at this point I wish to thank friends and family for sharing with me their favourite recipes. Special thanks go to Renee, Peter and Guy, and the gang at Paddock Farm, especially Alison, George and Victoria, who enthusiastically tasted beyond the call of duty. Thanks must also be extended to the National Dairy Council who happily provided me with boundless information on English and Welsh cheeses.

Introduction

A BRIEF HISTORY

Cheese in Britain has been made in a variety of ways since the Roman occupation, about 2,000 years ago. However, pots containing the remains of a type of cheese have been found dating back as far as 3000–2800 BC. Legend has it that cheese was discovered by accident when nomadic Arab tribesmen stored their milk in bags made of animals' stomachs, and hence discovered the end result of curdling milk with rennet. How cheese was actually made and the type of equipment used has not been established, but it is believed that cheesemaking itself closely followed the development of milking around the world.

Once this discovery was made, knowledge spread with travellers, crusaders and missionaries, and cheeses of many different types began to appear. In medieval Britain, cheese was made mainly on farms and in monasteries. For hundreds of years, up until the mid-1800s, British farmers, and especially the farmers' wives, traditionally made the cheese from unpasteurised milk from a small herd of cattle, thus establishing a unique British heritage. Today, about 90 per cent of all cheese manufactured in the UK is produced in creameries around the country. However, despite modern technology and mass production there are still farms producing cheese using the traditional methods and equipment.

NUTRITIONAL VALUE

Because cheese is a pure, concentrated form of milk, it contains most of the protein, vitamin A, calcium and fat of milk. Cheese is an essential part of our diet for protein and calcium. In fact, it contains more calcium than most other foods and is therefore a very important food for growing children, for pregnant mothers, and for strong teeth and bones. Cheese is also very valuable for vegetarians as an alternative to meat.

Here is a simple table supplied by the National Dairy Council showing the nutritional content of two popular cheeses:

Nutrient	Grams per 100g	
	Cheddar Cheese	Cottage Cheese
Protein	26.0	13.6
Fat	33.5	4.0
Carbohydrate	trace	1.4
Minerals	3.4	1.4
Water	37.0	78.8
Kilocalories } per (Kilojoules) } 100g	406 (1682)	96 (402)

SUCCESS WITH CHEESE

Buying

When it comes to choosing the best type of cheese to buy, it really is a matter of personal preference. Once you have made that decision, then you must make sure you are choosing the best quality cheese. If you have a very good cheesemonger nearby, you are very lucky, so make sure you use his good advice. The basic guideline is to buy cheese that looks fresh and not dry, and it is usually best to buy a piece cut from a whole cheese rather than one that is pre-packed. Carefully examine any labels, check the consistency of the rind and the fresh condition of the cheese. If buying pre-packed, make sure the cheese is not greasy or moist inside, check there is no mould and carefully check the 'sell-by' date.

A new scheme introduced by the National Dairy Council is called the English Cheese Mark. This grading system for English and Welsh cheeses is carried out by experienced creamery graders who assess batches of cheese, and if the batch is up to standard it will receive the mark of 'Quality Selected'. This scheme will provide you with an assurance that such cheeses will be of 'the finest, most consistent quality'.

Storing

Ideally, cheese should not be stored in conditions that are too cold. The best possible place to keep cheese is in a cool cellar, if you're lucky enough to have one, but if you are keeping it in the refrigerator, first protect it by placing it in a plastic bag that is set in an air-tight container. Place it in the least cold part of the refrigerator, at the bottom or in the door, at a temperature of 5–10°C/40–50°F. Never freeze cheese and never wrap different cheeses together as the flavours will mingle.

Serving

It is very important to eat cheese at the right temperature. If the cheese has been stored in the refrigerator, it should be allowed to reach room temperature (about 20°C/68°F) before eating. The time it takes to reach room temperature depends on the type of cheese and how cold a temperature it has been stored at.

Cooking with Cheese

Well, you can see for yourself in the following pages how different cheeses can be used in cooking in a variety of ways. Cheese can be melted for sauces and fondues, or baked in quiches and breads; grated and sprinkled on to soups, served at the end of cocktail sticks or grilled on toast; and soft cream cheese makes wonderful desserts – the possibilities are endless. Whatever you're making, always remember not to overcook cheese or it will become tough and stringy.

A DICTIONARY OF FAVOURITE CHEESES

British Cheeses

Caerphilly

Caerphilly, named after a village near Cardiff, first appeared in about 1831, and is the only true Welsh cheese. White, crumbly and smooth, and a little salty, it takes only 2 weeks to mature. A good eating cheese and excellent toasted.

Cheddar (Mature and Mild)

This golden, close, firm-textured cheese first appeared near Cheddar in Somerset at the beginning of the sixteenth century. It can be bought at all different stages of maturity, but the two most popular are the mild Cheddar, matured for 3–5 months, and mature Cheddar, matured for 5–12 months. A fine eating and cooking cheese.

Cheshire (Red, White and Blue)

The oldest of English cheeses, Cheshire can be traced back to the Romans and was mentioned in the Domesday book in 1086. Originally made near Cheshire, this slightly salty, mild cheese can only be made from the milk of cows grazed on the salty pastures in Cheshire or Shropshire. Always good, try the farmhouse Cheshire for the very best. Red and white (with no difference in flavour) are excellent, all-round cheeses. There is also a blue Cheshire which is salty and sharp with blue mould veins, but it is hard to find.

Cottage Cheese

A low-fat, white cheese made from skimmed cows' milk. It is good eaten fresh out of the tub and can be used in cooking, and as a substitute for Ricotta cheese. It can be bought in various flavours, for example, with chives, onion and pineapple.

Cream Cheese

This is a white, soft cheese made with cream which varies in fat content. It can be eaten fresh or used in cooking – excellent for cheesecakes.

Derby and Sage Derby

The production of Derby cheese is relatively small, mainly because it is a difficult cheese to produce. Factory production of this cheese began in 1870 in the first English cheese factory established at Longford, near Derby. Today, farmhouse production has ceased completely. Sage Derby is Derby cheese with sage leaves blended in to produce a green marbling effect and a slightly mild sage flavour. It is very attractive on a cheeseboard.

Gloucester (Double and Single)

Double Gloucester was originally made from the creamy milk of the Gloucester Black cows. This orange, strong yet mellow-flavoured cheese is matured for longer than the white, milder Single Gloucester. Today, Single Gloucester is made on only one farm in Gloucester and is rarely seen. Both can also be bought with additional flavours, such as chives, nuts and herbs.

Lancashire

Lancashire is a fairly soft, pressed cheese, crumbly and with plenty of flavour. Rich and creamy 'double curd' Lancashire is the more traditional and earns its name as the curd is made one day and then added to freshly-made curds the following day. Single curd is produced by most creameries and is the crumbly and drier of the two. An excellent melting cheese, ideal for cooking.

Leicester

Leicester is easily identifiable because of its reddish colour and is often called Red Leicester. It has a mellow flavour and is matured between 1–12 weeks. Another excellent melting cheese.

Stilton

Stilton rightly deserves all when it is referred to as 'The King of Cheeses'. It was first sold at the Bell Inn in Stilton Village, and the travellers on the Great North Road soon spread news of the unique, blue-veined cheese. Today, manufacture is tightly controlled by a certified trade mark ensuring that this cheese is only made in the counties of Derbyshire, Nottinghamshire and Leicestershire. White Stilton is simply a young version and rather more bland because the blue veining has not developed. A perfect eating and cooking cheese.

Wensleydale

This creamy white cheese with its refreshing flavour was originally produced by the Cistercian monks at Jervaulx Abbey, who came to England with William the Conqueror. They fled during the Dissolution of the Monasteries in the sixteenth century, leaving behind them the recipe for this cheese which soon spread to farmhouses and dairies. A blue-veined variety is also produced.

France

Brie

This is probably one of the most popular of all French cheeses, and the oldest, as it first appeared during the thirteenth century. Today, this cheese is not only made all over France but all over the world. When choosing Brie at its best, make sure the yellowish cheese is glossy, smooth and not too runny, and the white rind should be tender and firm. If the Brie is overripe it will smell of ammonia.

Camembert

Camembert first appeared in 1792 and is considered one of the great cheeses of Normandy. Today it is made all over the world, mostly using pasteurised milk, although in Normandy the best traditional cheese is still made with unpasteurised milk. Choose a cheese that is golden in colour with a smooth, cream-coloured rind and a fresh, clean smell. Avoid a cheese that is too runny.

Chèvre

This is a term used for goats' milk cheese, but there are many different types. In France, a law states that goats' milk cheese made entirely of goats' milk be called Chèvre and must contain at least 45 per cent fat. Any cheeses containing less fat and of a cows' and goats' milk mixture must be labelled 'mi-chèvre'.

Roquefort

This strong, salty, blue cheese is made from the milk of a breed of sheep known as Larzac and is matured in the Combalou Caves. All packets of this cheese show a picture of a sheep. Roquefort is wonderfully versatile and makes an excellent cheese for dessert.

Netherlands

Edam

This very familiar-looking cheese covered in a
bright red wax originated about 600 years ago in
the town of Edam. In the Netherlands, Edam is sold
in its natural golden-coloured rind, but is still easily
distinguishable by its spherical shape. Edam is only
made in cheese factories and is sold at different ages
of maturity and in different sizes. Its smooth
flavour makes it a wonderful eating and cooking
cheese, and its relatively low calories make it
popular with slimmers.

Gouda

This very important Dutch cheese first appeared in
the thirteenth century. Made from full milk, Gouda
ranges from a young, mild variety which is pale in
colour, to a more mature, fuller-flavoured cheese
with a spicy aroma. Gouda made from unpasteurised milk is clearly marked on the rind with the
word 'Boeren'. Gouda can be bought in different
sizes and is an ideal cooking cheese, no matter how
well matured.

Switzerland

Emmental

Emmental originated in the Emmen Valley and is
considered to be 'The Swiss Cheese'. Made from
unpasteurised milk, it is easily recognised by the
large holes throughout the golden cheese. It is an
extremely difficult cheese to produce, and one that
has not been truly reproduced anywhere else in the
world. An excellent eating and cooking cheese.

Gruyère

Gruyère originated in the twelfth century in the town of Gruyère. It is a pressed, cooked cheese, easily distinguishable with small holes and a reddish-brown rind. This is an excellent cooking cheese and the basis for such wonderful recipes as Swiss Fondue and Mornay Sauce.

Italy

Dolcelatte

This popular, blue-veined cheese is factory-made. It has a smooth, mild and delicate flavour that makes it an excellent eating cheese. Its name translated means 'sweet milk'.

Gorgonzola

Another Italian blue-veined cheese, Gorgonzola is sharper and spicier than Dolcelatte. It is believed to have originated over 1000 years ago and is regarded very highly around the world as a perfect eating cheese.

Mozzarella

Mozzarella is not a particularly interesting cheese when eaten on its own but becomes much tastier and of an interesting, stringy texture when melted, hence its international popularity melted on the top of pizza. Today Mozzarella is produced all over the world, but try and buy Italian Mozzarella for the best. An excellent way to enjoy this white cheese is the Italian way – sliced with plenty of olive oil, salt and pepper, fresh tomatoes and olives.

Parmesan

Too many of us have become accustomed to tasting Parmesan as a pre-packed powder. Also known as

Parmigiano Reggiano in Italy, when you eat this wonderful, yellowish, crumbly cheese fresh you'll never look back. The manufacturing of this cheese is tightly controlled and it can be bought at different stages of maturity. It is an excellent eating cheese when young, and a perfect cooking cheese when older.

Ricotta

Ricotta is a very popular cooking cheese in Italy. The cheese we buy today is a whey cheese, as it was traditionally, but sometimes it can be bought with added whole milk to give it a richer flavour. Ricotta is produced both very soft, also made with ewes' milk whey, and dried and hard enough to grate.

Greece

Feta (Fetta)

True Greek Feta cheese is still traditionally made with ewes' milk, although around the world it is produced with pasteurised milk. In Greece this cheese is still produced as it has been for thousands of years and is eaten in such large quantities that much of it has to be imported, mainly from Denmark. This white, salty cheese can either be bought crumbly or hard, and is excellent eaten in salads and for cooking.

Norway

Jarlsberg

This mellow, springy-textured cheese has become very popular, particularly in the United States, where great quantities are imported. It is very similar to Dutch Gouda and is made from pasteurised milk only in cheese factories. A very versatile cheese.

1
Party Appetisers

If you're organising a party, whether it be a large drinks do or a small intimate get-together, cheese can be your most important guest. This chapter gives just a small indication of the tremendous variety of 'little eats' you can prepare using your favourite cheeses. I could so easily have written a whole book on cheese appetisers – my imagination ran riot with hot and cold titbits, and I hope yours will do the same! Use a little invention of your own and try experimenting with different cheeses. Whether you serve a simple, varied cheeseboard, cheese cubes on cocktail sticks, or more elaborate hot and cold cheese dishes, your party is sure to be a success.

Stilton Fritters with Cumberland Sauce

**Serves 4
Preparation
time: 40
minutes**

This rather unusual party appetiser is quite a show-stopper when served with a Cumberland Sauce.

For the Cumberland Sauce:
1 orange
1 lemon
4 tablespoons redcurrant
  jelly
4 tablespoons port
2 teaspoons arrowroot
2 teaspoons water

For the fritters:
*450g/1lb Stilton cheese,
rind removed
1 egg
1 tablespoon milk
Salt and freshly-ground
  black pepper
25g/1oz plain flour
50g/2oz fresh breadcrumbs
Vegetable oil, for deep
  frying*

1　First make the sauce. Thinly pare the rind of both the orange and lemon and cut into very fine strips. Simmer for 5 minutes in a little water, remove from the heat and put aside.

2　Squeeze the orange and lemon juice into a saucepan and add the redcurrant jelly. Heat gently until the jelly has melted then simmer for 5 minutes. Add the port.

3　Blend together the arrowroot and water in a bowl and slowly stir in the redcurrant mixture. Pour back into the saucepan and stir over a gentle heat until the sauce has thickened and becomes clear. Drain the strips of orange and lemon rind and add to the sauce. Serve warm with the fritters.

4　To make the fritters, place the Stilton in the freezer until it is possible to cut finger-sized pieces without the cheese crumbling. In a bowl blend together the egg, milk and salt and pepper.

5 Coat each piece of cheese in the flour, dip in the egg mixture and roll in the breadcrumbs.

6 Heat the oil in a deep fryer to 180°C/350°F and fry the cheese until golden-brown. Drain on paper towels before serving.

Serving suggestion: Serve the warm fritters on a plate with a bowl of the warm sauce to dip them in.

Cheese Shortbread

These rich Gruyère biscuits also make a wonderful teatime treat.

Makes 4 triangles
Preparation time: 20 minutes
Cooking time: 25 minutes

3 tablespoons butter, softened
50g/2oz plain flour
¼ teaspoon salt

Pinch red pepper
1 egg yolk
50g/2oz finely-grated Gruyère cheese

Pre-heat the oven to 180°C/350°F/Gas Mark 4

1 In a bowl, cream the butter. Add the flour, salt and red pepper and blend together well. Add the egg yolk and blend until the dough forms a soft ball. Mix in the cheese thoroughly.

2 Place the dough on to a baking tray and using the back of a metal spoon, form into a 10cm/4in square about 1cm/½in thick. Using a sharp knife, cut diagonally into 4 even triangles and separate the triangles slightly with the knife. Bake for about 25 minutes or until golden. If the triangles join together again during cooking, separate them with the knife while still hot.

3 Cool on the baking tray for about 5 minutes then remove to a cooling rack.

Serving suggestion: Serve the shortbread while still warm.

Blue Cheese Whirls

Makes about 40
Preparation time: 40 minutes (plus freezing time)
Cooking time: 20–25 minutes

These whirls may take a little longer to make, so if you're pushed for time, prepare them up to a week in advance and keep securely wrapped in the refrigerator.

For the pastry:
225g/8oz plain flour
Generous pinch salt
50g/2oz unsalted butter
50g/2oz lard
1 egg yolk
Chilled water, to bind

For the filling:
275g/10oz blue cheese, well chilled
3 tablespoons dry sherry
150g/5oz very thinly-sliced ham
1 egg, beaten, to glaze

1 First make the pastry. Combine the flour and salt in a bowl. Add the butter and lard and chop into the flour using a cold knife. Rub in the fat until the mixture resembles fine breadcrumbs. Add the egg yolk and mix in thoroughly, then add enough chilled water to form a stiff dough. Knead together to form a ball, wrap in clingfilm and chill for at least 1 hour.

2 Place the blue cheese in a blender or food processor and process until smooth. Beat in the sherry.

3 Divide the pastry in half. Roll out one half on a floured surface to a 40 × 20cm/16 × 8in rectangle. Spread half the cheese mixture evenly over the top leaving a border around the edge. Cover with half the ham. From one long side roll the pastry as for a Swiss roll. Place on a baking tray. Repeat with the remaining pastry and cheese and ham. Cover and freeze for about 45 minutes.

Preheat the oven to 200°C/400°F/Gas Mark 6

4 Slice the pastry rolls into 1cm/½in slices and place the slices on a lightly-buttered baking tray. Brush with the beaten egg and bake for about 12–15 minutes until bubbly. Turn the baking trays around in the oven and bake for a further 8–10 minutes, until light brown. Transfer to a serving platter.

Serving suggestion: Allow the whirls to cool for about 5 minutes before serving.

Mozzarella Fritters

Smoked Mozzarella is also known as 'Mozzarella Affumicata' and can be found in most good cheese shops.

Makes about 24
Preparation time: 30 minutes
Cooking time: 20 minutes

225ml/8fl oz water
½ teaspoon salt
Pinch cayenne pepper
6 tablespoons unsalted butter
100g/4oz plain flour
4 eggs

100g/4oz smoked Mozzarella cheese, grated
2 tablespoons freshly-chopped parsley
Vegetable oil, for deep frying
Parsley sprigs, to garnish

1 Place the water, salt, pepper and butter together in a saucepan and bring to the boil. Remove from the heat, add the flour and beat together until the mixture is smooth. Place the saucepan back over a medium heat and continue to beat the mixture until it leaves the side of the pan, about 1 minute. Remove and allow to cool.

2 Make a well in the centre of the mixture and add 1 egg at a time, beating the batter until very smooth. Add the cheese and chopped parsley.

Pre-heat the oven to 100°C/200°F/Gas Mark Low

3 Place a single layer of paper towels in the base of a baking tray.

4 In a deep frying pan or wok, heat the oil to 170°C/325°F. Add large teaspoons of the mixture to the hot oil and cook until the fritters are golden and puffed, turning occasionally. Drain on paper towels then keep warm in the oven while continuing to cook the remainder of the mixture.

Serving suggestion: Serve the fritters hot and garnished with parsley sprigs.

Tiny Little Spinach Quiches

Makes about 34
Preparation time: 35 minutes
Cooking time: 25 minutes

These little hot canapés are so easy to serve and eat they are ideal for any busy drinks party.

For the shortcrust pastry:
175g/6oz plain flour
75g/3oz half butter, half lard
Pinch of salt
Cold water, to combine

For the filling:
150g/5oz frozen chopped spinach, thawed and drained
50g/2oz Gruyère cheese, grated
50ml/2fl oz single cream
50ml/2fl oz milk
2 eggs
Pinch of salt
Freshly-grated Parmesan cheese, for topping

1 First make the pastry. Place the flour and salt in a bowl and cut in the butter and lard. Rub the mixture together until it resembles fine breadcrumbs. Add enough cold water to combine to a stiff dough. Knead the pastry into a ball, cover with foil and chill for 30 minutes.

2   Lightly grease and flour 34 deep patty tins. On a lightly-floured board roll out the pastry to about 0.3cm/⅛in thickness. Using a 5cm/2in fluted pastry cutter, cut out rounds and line the patty tins with the pastry rounds.

Pre-heat the oven to 200°C/400°F/Gas Mark 6

3   Divide the spinach between the pastry shells and sprinkle each with a little grated cheese. In a bowl beat together the cream, milk, eggs and salt and spoon about 1 tablespoon of the cream mixture into each pastry shell. Bake in the hot oven for about 25 minutes or until a cake tester inserted into the centre comes out clean.

Serving suggestion: These little quiches can be served warm or cold.

Cheese-Wrapped Olives

These delicious deep-fried fritters are guaranteed to disappear before your very eyes.

Makes 25
Preparation time: 20 minutes (plus standing and refrigeration time)
Cooking time: 15 minutes

25g/1oz plain flour
½ teaspoon salt
Pinch freshly-ground black pepper
1 teaspoon dry yeast
350g/12oz Cheddar cheese, grated
3 egg yolks

50ml/2fl oz beer
2 egg whites
Pinch cream of tartar
25 large Spanish olives
Plain flour, for coating
Vegetable oil, for deep frying

1   In a bowl combine together the flour, salt, pepper and yeast. Add the cheese.

2   In another small bowl mix together the egg yolks and the beer. Add to the dry ingredients and beat until smooth.

3 In a third bowl beat together the egg whites and the cream of tartar until stiff but not dry. Fold into the batter. Allow the mixture to stand for about 1 hour 30 minutes then cover and refrigerate for another hour.

4 Pat the olives dry. Around each olive mould about 1 tablespoon of the batter then coat each with flour.

5 Heat the oil in a deep saucepan to a temperature of 190°C/375°F. Deep fry the olive fritters in batches until golden-brown all over, about 3 minutes. Drain on paper towels.

Serving suggestion: Serve these fritters immediately while they are still warm.

Cheese Spread with Cumin

The combination of flavours in this cheese spread is quite unique, highlighted by the wonderful accent of the toasted cumin seeds.

Makes about 275g/10oz
Preparation time: 15 minutes

1 teaspoon cumin seeds
175g/6oz goat cheese, at room temperature
175g/6oz mild Cheddar

50g/2oz unsalted butter, at room temperature
Melba toasts, to serve

1   Place the cumin seeds in a heavy-based frying pan and cook over a high heat, shaking the seeds occasionally, until aromatic but not brown – about 3 minutes. Remove from the heat.

2   Put the goat cheese in a blender or food processor. Chop the Cheddar into cubes and add to the goat cheese. Add the cumin seeds and blend until very smooth – about 2 minutes. Serve at room temperature with Melba toast.

Serving suggestion: This cheese spread may be prepared a week in advance if kept in an air-tight container in the refrigerator.

Fried Cheddar Cheese Chips

Nobody can resist these delicious Cheddar cheese chips. They're wonderful to make for children's parties too.

Makes about 30
Preparation time: 20 minutes
Cooking time: 5 minutes

350g/12oz mature Cheddar cheese
225ml/8fl oz warm milk
65g/2½ oz plain flour
Pinch cayenne pepper
2 eggs

50g/2oz dry breadcrumbs
Salt and freshly-ground black pepper
Vegetable oil, for deep frying

1 Using a sharp knife, cut the cheese into 4 × 2½cm/1½ × 1in sticks. Place in a bowl with the warm milk and leave the cheese to soak for about 10 minutes.

2 Combine the flour and cayenne pepper. Drain the cheese sticks and coat completely in the flour. Beat the eggs in another bowl and dip the flour-coated cheese in the egg.

3 Season the breadcrumbs with the salt and pepper and dip the cheese into the breadcrumbs to coat completely.

4 In a large saucepan heat the oil to 190°C/375°F. Add the cheese sticks in batches and deep fry until golden-brown, about 15 seconds. Drain on paper towels before serving.

Serving suggestion: Serve these cheese chips warm.

Aubergine Packages

Makes about 16
Preparation time: See recipe
Cooking time: 20 minutes

You may choose whichever blue cheese you prefer for this recipe although I do recommend using Roquefort.

One 450g/1lb aubergine, peeled
2 cloves garlic, crushed
125ml/4fl oz olive oil
2 teaspoons dried mixed herbs (see note)
Large pinch freshly-ground black pepper

3 firm tomatoes
100g/4oz blue cheese, cut into little pieces
32 whole, fresh basil leaves
Finely-chopped basil leaves, to garnish

1 Cut the aubergine lengthwise into ½cm/¼in slices. Sprinkle with a little salt and leave to drain for at least 2 hours.

Pre-heat the oven to 190°C/375°F/Gas Mark 5

2 Pat the aubergine dry with paper towels and place in a single layer on a baking tray lined with greaseproof paper.

3 In a bowl whisk together the garlic, oil, herbs and pepper. Brush this mixture lightly over the aubergine and bake for about 20 minutes or until the aubergine browns around the edges. Brush again with the oil and leave to cool.

4 Cut the tomatoes into julienne (very thin strips). Arrange the tomato and cheese over one short end of each aubergine slice. Place 2 fresh basil leaves on top and roll up the aubergine, starting at the end with the filling. Arrange on a serving platter, seam side down, and garnish with chopped basil. Serve at room temperature.

Note: The best mixed herbs to use for this recipe are *herbes de Provence* which can be found in most delicatessens.

Bacon Spinach Balls

Here's a very quick appetiser to make. You can prepare them beforehand, then cook just before serving so they're still warm.

Makes about 32
Preparation time: 15 minutes
Cooking time: About 15 minutes

275g/10oz package frozen, chopped spinach, thawed
40g/1½oz freshly-grated Parmesan cheese
175g/6oz dry breadcrumbs
25g/1oz crisp, cooked bacon, crumbled

Pinch garlic powder
Pinch freshly-ground black pepper
50g/2oz butter, melted
3 eggs
Vegetable oil, for shallow frying

1 First squeeze all the water out of the frozen spinach.

2   In a large bowl combine the spinach, cheese, breadcrumbs, bacon, garlic powder and pepper. Add the melted butter and the eggs and mix together well.

3   Roll the spinach mixture into even-sized 2cm/1in balls. Heat the oil in a heavy-based frying pan and fry the balls in batches until golden-brown all over – about 2 minutes. Drain on paper towels before serving. Serve warm.

Serving suggestion: If you need to reheat the Bacon Spinach Balls for serving, simply place on a baking tray and reheat in an oven set at 190°C/ 375°F/Gas Mark 5 for about 5 minutes.

Greek Phyllo Rolls

**Makes 72
Preparation
time: 40
minutes
Cooking time:
15 minutes**

This recipe is ideal for a large party. The rolls are perfect for serving as they can be eaten either hot or cold.

*1 tablespoon olive oil
50g/2oz finely-chopped
   onion
275g/10oz package frozen
chopped spinach, thawed
225g/8oz cottage cheese*

*100g/4oz cream cheese
100g/4oz Feta cheese
1 egg, lightly beaten
12 sheets phyllo pastry
225g/8oz butter, melted*

1   First heat the oil in a large saucepan over a medium heat and sauté the onion until translucent – about 2 to 3 minutes. Reduce the heat and add the spinach. Slowly add the cheeses and blend together well. Add the egg and mix together.

2   Stack 3 of the pastry sheets on a damp tea cloth. Butter a large baking tray with some of the melted butter. Brush each of the stacked pastry sheets with a little melted butter and restack.

3 Spoon about 100g/4oz of the cheese mixture into a 4cm/1½in wide strip down the long side of the stacked pastry and starting at the long edge with the filling, roll up as for a Swiss roll using the tea cloth for help. Place carefully in the buttered baking tray, seam side down.

4 Repeat with the remaining phyllo to make 3 more rolls. Place in the freezer for about 15 minutes.

Pre-heat the oven to 180°C/350°F/Gas Mark 4

5 Cut the prepared rolls into 2½cm/1in pieces. Place on the baking tray and cook until golden, about 15 minutes.

Serving suggestion: These rolls may be served hot or cold.

Goat Cheese Crackers

Perfect little appetisers to serve with drinks! These crackers will keep for up to 2 days in an airtight container.

Makes about 36
Preparation time: 15 minutes
Cooking time: 8 minutes

100g/4oz unsalted butter, softened
100g/4oz goat cheese, at room temperature
2 tablespoons freshly-grated Parmesan cheese

100g/4oz plain flour
½ teaspoon salt
Pinch of cayenne pepper

Pre-heat the oven to 190°C/375°F/Gas Mark 5

1 Place the butter and both cheeses into a blender or food processor and blend until smooth. Add the remaining ingredients and process until just blended.

2 Place the cheese mixture into a piping bag fitted with a star-shaped nozzle and pipe 5cm/2in strips on to an ungreased baking tray.

3 Place in the oven and bake until the edges are just beginning to brown, about 8 minutes. Allow the crackers to cool on a cooling rack then store in an airtight container until ready to serve.

Fried Brie

Serves 8–10
Preparation time: 15 minutes (plus chilling)
Cooking time: 15 minutes

This delicious appetiser should be served immediately while still hot and soft. The Brie can be prepared for cooking up to 8 hours ahead if kept covered in the refrigerator.

1 egg, lightly beaten
1 tablespoon water
100g/4oz dry breadcrumbs
Salt and freshly-ground black pepper
25g/1oz freshly-grated Parmesan cheese

450g/1lb wheel Brie cheese
50ml/2fl oz vegetable oil, for frying
Slices of French bread, to serve

1 In a bowl combine together the egg and water. In another bowl combine the breadcrumbs with some salt and pepper and the Parmesan cheese.

2 Dip the Brie wheel in the egg mixture, coating completely, then coat in the breadcrumb mixture. Cover and chill for at least 1 hour.

3 Heat the oil in a large frying pan. Add the Brie and cook until browned on both sides and softened – about 2 minutes on each side.

Serving suggestion: Serve the hot Brie on a dish with slices of French bread.

Baked Brie with Garlic

For garlic lovers everywhere . . . this wonderful cheese appetiser is excellent at the start of any dinner party.

Serves 8
Preparation time: 15 minutes
Cooking time: About 1 hour 30 minutes

4 large cloves garlic
50ml/2fl oz olive oil
1 teaspoon salt

4 × 100g/4oz rounds Brie
Slices French bread,
*   toasted, to serve*

Pre-heat the oven to 180°F/350°C/Gas Mark 4

1   Using a sharp knife, very carefully remove the outer skins of the garlic cloves, leaving one layer of skin. Arrange the cloves in a small baking dish, drizzle with the oil and sprinkle with the salt.

2   Cover the dish with foil and bake until the garlic is very tender, about 1 hour 30 minutes.

3   Heat the grill to 'high'. Using a sharp knife, score a cross in the top of each Brie round. Place each round in a baking dish and place under the grill until brown and bubbly – about 5 minutes.

Serving suggestion: Serve the hot cheeses immediately with the roasted garlic and toasted slices of French bread.

Nutty Cheese Wafers

Cheese and nuts always make a popular combination. If you can't find pecan nuts, try this recipe using walnuts instead.

Makes about 60
Preparation time: 20 minutes (plus chilling)
Cooking time: 15 minutes

225g/8oz Cheddar cheese,
*   grated*
175g/6oz plain flour
100g/4oz butter, softened

½ teaspoon salt
Pinch cayenne pepper
50g/2oz chopped pecan
*   nuts*

1 Put the cheese, flour, butter, salt and cayenne pepper in a large bowl. Using an electric mixer, combine the ingredients well. Add the chopped nuts and mix in thoroughly.

2 Divide the mixture into three equal quantities and form each into a log shape. Wrap each in greaseproof paper and clingfilm and chill for at least 1 hour until firm.

Pre-heat the oven to 170°C/325°F/Gas Mark 3

3 Cut the dough mixture into 5mm/¼in slices and arrange the slices on a baking tray about 4cm/1½in apart. Bake for about 15 minutes until golden-brown. Cool completely on paper towels. Either serve immediately or store in an air-tight container.

Note: The dough for these cheese wafers can be prepared 3 days in advance if kept in the refrigerator, or 2 months in advance if kept frozen.

Cheese Crescents

**Makes about 24
Preparation time: 1 hour
Cooking time: About 15 minutes**

These delicious little crescents combine an international festival of flavours – Feta cheese from Greece and Mozzarella from Italy.

For the pastry:
*200g/7oz wholewheat flour
150g/5oz plain flour
Large pinch salt
½ teaspoon baking powder
175g/6oz butter, softened
Cold water, to combine*

For the filling:
*1 large onion, very finely minced
225g/8oz Feta cheese, crumbled
100g/4oz Mozzarella cheese, grated
2 eggs, beaten
125ml/4fl oz olive oil, for frying*

1 First make the pastry. In a bowl combine both flours, salt and baking powder. Add the butter and rub into the flour until the mixture resembles fine breadcrumbs. Add just enough cold water to combine to a dough.

2 Knead the dough on a floured surface until smooth, then cover in clingfilm and chill for about 30 minutes.

3 For the filling, combine the onion and both cheeses in a bowl. Add the eggs and combine together well.

4 Divide the dough into walnut-sized balls and roll out each ball to a 15cm/6in round. Place a rounded tablespoon of the cheese filling in the centre on each pastry round and fold in half. Seal the edges with the back of a fork.

5 Heat the olive oil in a heavy-based frying pan to 180°C/350°F. Cook the pastries in batches for about 2−3 minutes or until light brown on both sides. Drain on paper towels before serving warm.

Note: You can prepare these crescents 1 day in advance if they are kept covered in the refrigerator. Simply reheat in the oven for about 5 minutes and serve warm.

Chilli Balls

Makes about 30
Preparation time: 25 minutes (plus chilling)
Cooking time: See recipe

Serve these spicy cheese balls immediately while still hot.

225g/8oz Cheddar cheese, grated
175g/6oz uncooked prawns, trimmed and finely chopped
1½ tablespoons fresh coriander, finely chopped
1 tablespoon finely-chopped chilli pepper
Pinch of chilli powder

For the batter:
Vegetable oil, for deep frying
100g/4oz plain flour
Pinch of salt
50g/2oz cornflour
¾ teaspoon baking powder
225ml/8fl oz water
2 tablespoons vegetable oil
Fresh breadcrumbs for coating

1   First mix together in a bowl the cheese, prawns, coriander, chilli and chilli powder and combine well. Roll into small balls and put aside.

2   Heat the oil in a deep fryer to 180°C/350°F. In a large bowl combine the flour, salt, cornflour and baking powder. Make a well in the middle and add the water and the 2 tablespoons oil. Whisk into the flour mixture gradually until a smooth batter forms.

3   Dip each cheese ball into the batter and allow any excess to drip off. Roll in the breadcrumbs to coat thoroughly then deep fry in small batches until golden-brown. Drain the cheese balls on paper towels before serving. Serve immediately.

Serving suggestion: You may like to make your favourite Oriental dip to accompany these cheese balls.

Cheese Pastry Triangles

Here's a very simple treat that I've found more than one use for! Try serving them with home-made apple pie for dessert – they make a wonderful combination.

Makes 6
Preparation time: 15 minutes
Cooking time: About 12 minutes

225g/8oz frozen puff pastry, thawed
25g/1oz Cheddar cheese, grated

1 egg beaten with 1 tablespoon water
25g/1oz freshly-grated Parmesan cheese

Pre-heat the oven to 230°C/450°F/Gas Mark 8

1   Lightly grease a baking tray.

2   On a lightly-floured board, roll out the pastry to a thickness of ½cm/¼in. Sprinkle over the Cheddar cheese evenly, then gently run a rolling pin over to press in the cheese. Brush with the beaten egg and water glaze.

3   Using a sharp knife or a pastry cutter, cut out 6 even triangles. Sprinkle the top with the Parmesan cheese and arrange on the baking tray.

4   Place in the centre of the oven and bake for about 12 minutes, until golden-brown.

Serving suggestion: These pastries are best if served warm from the oven.

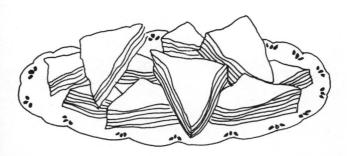

Of Mice and Men

Serves 8
Preparation time: 10 minutes
Grilling time: 2 minutes

These whirls may take a little longer to make, so if you're pushed for time, prepare them up to a week in advance and keep securely wrapped in the refrigerator.

2 pitta breads
25g/1oz butter
8 canned asparagus spears, drained

2 tomatoes
50g/2oz Cheddar cheese, grated

1   First cut each pitta bread in half to form 4 pockets.

2   Butter the inside of each pocket. Arrange the asparagus spears neatly in each pocket.

3   Slice the tomatoes very thinly and arrange inside the pockets.

4   Cover the top of each pocket with the grated cheese. Place under a medium grill for about 2 minutes, until the cheese has melted and is bubbling. Remove from the grill and cut each pitta pocket in half. Serve at once.

Serving suggestion: This combination of filling can make a substantial luncheon dish also. Instead of cutting the pitta breads into 2, simply slit each bread horizontally along the edge, keeping it intact. Fill each bread with the ingredients suggested above and add some shredded lettuce if you like. Cook as above and serve immediately.

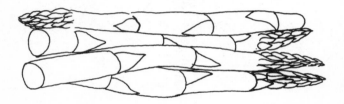

2
Salads and Luncheon Dishes

When it comes to salads, cheese is a must. No matter what time of year or what salad ingredients are available, there's a cheese to suit every combination. Luncheon dishes cover a whole spectrum of recipes, from the light ladies' get-together, to the outdoor picnic, to the more substantial family gathering, and cheese most certainly proves its versatility here in this chapter. With hot and cold dishes, some quick and easy recipes and some a little more complicated (but I hope all exciting), this collection will help you make the most of your cheese favourites.

Gruyère Tart

Serves 8
Preparation
time: 2 hours
Cooking time:
40 minutes

This creamy, rich tart is perfect to serve at any special luncheon

For the pastry:
175g/6oz plain flour
Pinch of salt
75g/3oz unsalted butter,
chilled
3–4 tablespoons warm
water

For the filling:
150g/5oz Gruyère cheese,
grated
225ml/8fl oz crème fraîche
2 eggs
Salt and freshly-ground
black pepper
Freshly-grated nutmeg
50g/2oz butter

1   First make the pastry. Combine the flour and salt in a bowl. Add the butter cut in several pieces and rub into the flour until the mixture resembles fine breadcrumbs. Stir in just enough warm water to mix to a soft dough. Wrap the dough in clingfilm and refrigerate for at least 1 hour.

2   Lightly butter a 20cm/8in pie plate. Carefully roll the dough out to fit the prepared pie plate. Line the pie plate with the pastry, trim the edges and chill for a further 30 minutes.

Pre-heat the oven to 220°C/425°F/Gas Mark 7

3   Bake the pastry shell blind with foil for about 10 minutes, then remove the foil and bake for a further 8 minutes or until the crust is lightly browned.

4   Reduce the oven to 190°C/375°F/Gas Mark 5. Sprinkle the grated cheese over the base of the pie shell. In a bowl mix together the crème fraîche and the eggs. Add salt, pepper and nutmeg to taste. Pour over the cheese and dot the top with butter.

5   Bake for 35 to 30 minutes until set. Make sure the pastry does not brown too quickly (*see* note), and leave the tart to stand for 5 minutes before serving.

Note: Cover the rim of the pastry with foil if it begins to brown too quickly.

Quick and Easy Pizza

Although the filling and dough for this pizza are made a day ahead of cooking, this recipe is so easy I'm sure you'll get hooked on making your own.

Makes one 40cm/16in pizza
Preparation time: Prepare one day ahead
Cooking time: 25 minutes

For the pizza dough:
1 envelope dry yeast
1 teaspoon sugar
225ml/8fl oz warm water
1 tablespoon sunflower oil
1 teaspoon salt
350g/12oz plain flour
225g/8oz mushrooms,
  sliced

For the filling:
5 tomatoes, peeled, seeds
  removed and chopped
450g/1lb Mozzarella
  cheese, chopped
175ml/6fl oz olive oil
4 cloves garlic, crushed
1 bunch fresh basil,
  chopped
Salt and freshly-ground
  black pepper

1   In a large bowl combine together the tomatoes, cheese, oil, garlic and basil. Season to taste with salt and pepper and cover the bowl with cling-film. Leave in the refrigerator overnight.

2   To prepare the pizza dough, sprinkle the yeast and sugar over the warm water in a bowl. Stir until dissolved then leave until the mixture becomes foamy, about 5 minutes. Add the oil and salt and stir in enough flour, a little at a time, to make a soft dough.

3   Place the dough on a lightly-floured surface and knead until smooth and elastic. Seal in a plastic bag and refrigerate overnight.

4   Have the dough at room temperature.

Pre-heat the oven to 200°C/400°F/Gas Mark 6

5   Lightly oil a 40cm/16in pizza pan. Roll out the dough to fit the pan, cover with a tea towel and leave to rise in a warm temperature for about 20 minutes. Bake in the oven for 5 minutes.

6   Arrange the cheese filling evenly over the crust and sprinkle the top with the mushrooms. Return to the oven and bake until the edges are just brown, about 20 minutes. Serve immediately.

Serving suggestion: Try any of your favourite ingredients as a filling for this pizza. The possibilities are endless!

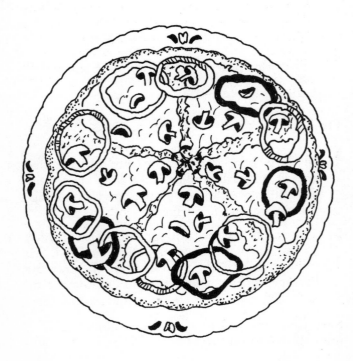

Scalloped Cheese, Onion and Ham Bake

This recipe also makes a delicious but simple brunch dish.

Serves 4–6
Preparation time: 40 minutes
Cooking time: 35 minutes

75g/3oz butter
1125g/2½lb onions, sliced
1 teaspoon sugar
Salt
50g/2oz fresh breadcrumbs
350g/12oz smoked ham, cut into thin slices

200g/7oz Emmental cheese, grated
Freshly-ground black pepper
Freshly-grated nutmeg
450ml/16fl oz whipping cream, scalded

1 Melt 50g/2oz of the butter in a frying pan and cook the onions until softened, stirring, for about 10 minutes. Add the sugar and continue to cook for about 5 minutes until the onions are light brown. Season to taste with salt.

2 Put the remaining butter in another frying pan and fry the breadcrumbs for about 5 minutes, until golden-brown.

Pre-heat the oven to 190°C/375°F/Gas Mark 5

3 Place half the onions in the base of a baking dish. Top with half the ham and half the cheese. Season with salt and pepper and nutmeg, then repeat the layers with the remaining onions, ham and cheese. Pour the cream over the top and sprinkle with the breadcrumbs.

4 Bake for about 35 minutes until it is lightly browned and bubbly, and the cream is absorbed.

Serving suggestion: Leave to stand for about 15 minutes before serving.

Stuffed Peppers

Serves 4
Preparation
time: 30
minutes
Cooking time:
30 minutes

I have to thank the National Dairy Council for this attractive and healthy luncheon treat.

4 medium-sized red and green peppers
50g/2oz pasta shells
2 carrots, sliced
1 courgette, sliced
50g/2oz butter
1 onion, thinly sliced

40g/1 ½oz plain flour
Pinch mustard powder
275ml/½ pint milk
225g/8oz Red Leicester cheese, grated
Salt and freshly-ground black pepper

1   Cut each pepper across the top, reserve the lids and remove all the seeds and pith. Rinse and pat dry. Blanch the peppers in boiling, salted water and drain on paper towels.

2   Cook the pasta according to the instructions on the packet. Blanch the celery and carrots for about 3 minutes, adding the courgette just for the last minute.

Pre-heat the oven to 180°C/350°F/Gas Mark 4

3   Melt the butter in a saucepan, add the onion and fry until soft. Add the flour and mustard, stir in well, then add the milk very gradually, stirring continuously. Bring to the boil, stir in the pasta, vegetables and 175g/6oz of the cheese. Season with salt and pepper and spoon equal amounts of filling into each pepper shell. Sprinkle with the remaining grated cheese and place in an ovenproof dish.

4   Bake in the oven for about 30 minutes. Replace the tops of the peppers and serve immediately.

Serving suggestion: Serve the stuffed peppers with a crisp, green salad.

Fresh Spinach Salad

Choose young, tender spinach for this hearty salad.

Serves 4–6
Preparation time: 20 minutes

2 cloves garlic, halved
1 bunch lightly-cooked
  broccoli
225g/8oz fresh spinach
1 head crisp lettuce
175g/6oz can tuna,
  drained
8 cherry tomatoes, halved
Crisp, cooked bacon,
  chopped (optional)

**For the Parmesan
  salad dressing:**
75ml/3fl oz olive oil
25g/1oz freshly-grated
  Parmesan cheese
1½ tablespoons fresh
  lemon juice
1½ tablespoons fresh lime
  juice

1 First rub the cut side of the garlic around the inside of a large wooden salad bowl. Discard the garlic.

2 Cut the broccoli into florets and put in the bowl. Shred the spinach and lettuce and add to the bowl. Add the tuna and the halved cherry tomatoes. Add the chopped, crisp bacon if you are using it.

3 To make the salad dressing, place all the ingredients in a small bowl and whisk together thoroughly. Pour over the salad, toss well and serve immediately.

Note: The salad dressing can be made in advance but do be sure to whisk it once again before pouring it over the salad and tossing.

Apple and Gorgonzola Salad

Gorgonzola, the wonderful blue-veined cheese from Italy, is an excellent companion to the sweet, crisp apples in this salad.

Serves 6
Preparation time: 20 minutes

1 curly endive
50g/2oz Gorgonzola
   cheese, crumbled
Salt and freshly-ground
   black pepper

For the dressing:
175ml/6fl oz whipping
   cream
3 tablespoons red wine
   vinegar
4 large, crisp green apples

1   First make the salad dressing. In a bowl combine together the cream and vinegar. Peel and core the apples and cut into thin slices. Add the apple slices to the cream mixture and mix together well. Put aside while making the salad.

2   Remove the stems of the endive and tear the leaves into bite-sized pieces. Place in a bowl and add the Gorgonzola and the apple mixture. Toss well so the creamy dressing coats the whole salad. Season with salt and pepper to taste and serve immediately.

Note: You can make the creamy apple dressing up to 1 hour before serving.

Chicken Liver Quiche

Serves 6–8
Preparation time: 35 minutes
Cooking time: 35 minutes

If you love chicken livers, you'll adore this rich, tasty quiche.

One 23cm/9in pie crust
2 tablespoons wholegrain
   mustard
6 large mushrooms, sliced
1 onion, sliced
175g/6oz chicken livers
75ml/3fl oz soured cream
2 tablespoons sherry
Salt and freshly-ground
   black pepper

50g/2oz Cheddar cheese,
   grated
3 tablespoons freshly-
   grated Parmesan cheese
3 eggs
350ml/12fl oz whipping
   cream
Pinch of sugar
Pinch of cayenne pepper

1   Prepare your favourite shortcrust pastry and line a 23cm/9in pie dish.

Pre-heat the oven to 220°C/425°F/Gas Mark 7

2   Brush the base of the pie shell with the mustard and bake for 5 minutes. Keep the oven at this temperature.

3   Melt the butter in a saucepan, add the mushroom and onion and cook until just tender. Add the livers and cook for 1 minute, then reduce the heat and cook for 15 minutes, covered.

4   Add the soured cream and sherry and stir until thoroughly heated. Season with salt and pepper and spoon the mixture into the pie shell. Sprinkle the cheese over the top.

5   Whip the eggs lightly then add the cream, sugar and cayenne and blend well. Pour over the cheese and bake for 15 minutes. Reduce the temperature to 200°C/400°F/Gas Mark 6 and continue cooking until a cake tester inserted into the centre comes out clean – about 20 minutes.

Serving suggestion: Allow the quiche to cool for 5 minutes before serving.

Welsh Rabbit

Serves 4
Preparation time: 25 minutes

An amusing and delicious alternative to a traditional favourite.

2 tablespoons butter
450g/1lb mature Cheddar cheese, grated
½ teaspoon mustard
1 tablespoon Worcestershire sauce
Pinch cayenne pepper

2 eggs, lightly beaten
125ml/4fl oz single cream
2 baps, split in half and toasted
4 slices bacon, cooked
4 slices tomato

1 In a large saucepan melt the butter, add the cheese and stir until the cheese has melted. Stir in the Worcestershire sauce, mustard and cayenne. Remove from the heat.

2 In a small bowl combine the eggs and cream. Stir into the cheese mixture until well blended. Return to the heat and cook, stirring, until thickened.

3 Place one bap half on each serving plate and top each with a slice of bacon and a slice of tomato. Spoon equal amounts of the 'rabbit' mixture over each. Place under a hot grill for 1 minute to heat through and serve immediately.

Serving suggestion: Serve these rabbits with fresh salad.

French Boats

Serves 4
Preparation time: 20 minutes

Here's a quick and wholesome luncheon that everyone will enjoy. Although I have suggested you use Cheshire cheese, you really can use any cheese you like.

225g/8oz Cheshire cheese,
   grated
100g/4oz ham, diced
100g/4oz button
   mushrooms, diced
2 teaspoons wholegrain
   mustard

4 egg yolks
Salt and freshly-ground
   black pepper
Pinch of paprika
2 × 20cm/8in French
   loaves

1   In a bowl combine together the cheese, ham, diced mushrooms, mustard and egg yolks. Season with salt and pepper to taste and add the paprika.

2   Slice the two French loaves in half lengthwise. Using a spoon, scoop out the soft bread to make a cavity about 2.5cm/1in deep (*see* note).

3   Spoon equal amounts of cheese filling into the cavities and spread evenly in the 'boats'.

4   Heat a grill to 'hot' and grill the boats until the cheese has melted and is bubbling, about 3 minutes. Serve immediately with a side salad.

Note: Don't throw away the soft inside of the bread. Save it for croûtons or breadcrumbs – you never know when you'll need it!

Cold Brie Omelettes

Here's a rather different type of omelette that's ideal for taking on a picnic.

**Serves 8
Preparation
time: 5
minutes
Cooking time:
15 minutes**

9 eggs
1 tablespoon finely-
   chopped fresh parsley
1 tablespoon finely-
   chopped fresh chervil

1 tablespoon finely-
   chopped fresh chives
Salt and freshly-ground
   black pepper
100g/4oz Brie
75g/3oz butter

1   In a bowl combine together three of the eggs, one-third of the herbs and salt and pepper. Beat together lightly with a fork.

2   Cut the Brie into 3 pieces. Take one piece and dice. Place a heavy-based 15cm/6in frying pan over a medium heat and add 2 tablespoons of the butter. Heat until no longer foaming, making sure the base and sides of the pan are thoroughly coated. Add the egg mixture and tilt so the egg coats the pan.

3   Cook the egg mixture until almost set and sprinkle the diced Brie over the top. Reduce the heat and cook until the Brie is melted. Roll the omelette as you would for a Swiss roll and transfer to a plate.

4   Repeat with the remaining ingredients to make 2 more omelettes. Chill before serving, then cut into 2.5cm/1in slices. Serve at room temperature.

Serving suggestion: Serve the Brie omelettes with plenty of fresh salad.

Gruyère and Ham Salad with Roquefort Dressing

Here's a wonderfully hearty salad for any large lunch or dinner party.

Serves 12–14
Preparation time: 20 minutes

For the Roquefort dressing:
125ml/4fl oz red wine vinegar
1 tablespoon wholegrain mustard
1 clove garlic, crushed
350ml/12fl oz olive oil
40g/1½oz Roquefort cheese, crumbled

675g/1½lb cabbage, shredded
350g/12oz ham, cut into julienne strips
350g/12oz Gruyère cheese, cut into julienne strips
6 tablespoons finely-chopped fresh parsley
Salt and freshly-ground black pepper
1 large crisp lettuce

1   First make the salad dressing. Blend together in a large bowl the vinegar, mustard and crushed garlic. Add the olive oil slowly, whisking continuously. Stir in the cheese until smooth.

2   Just before serving, add the cabbage, ham and Gruyère cheese to the prepared dressing with 4 tablespoons of the chopped parsley. Season with salt and pepper and combine together well.

3   Arrange the crisp lettuce leaves on a serving platter and spoon the ham and cheese salad into the centre. Sprinkle the remaining parsley over the top and serve immediately.

Note: If you wish you can prepare the salad dressing before adding the Gruyère and ham 1 day in advance of serving. Keep well covered in the refrigerator.

Cold Macaroni Salad

**Serves 4
Preparation
time: 30
minutes**

Fresh buttermilk can be found in most good health food shops.

*225g/8oz macaroni
225g/8oz thinly-sliced
ham
175g/6oz Edam cheese,
cubed
250g/9oz seedless grapes
40g/1½oz celery, chopped
½ ripe honeydew melon
Small head crisp lettuce*

**For the buttermilk
salad dressing:**
*125ml/4fl oz buttermilk
125ml/4fl oz mayonnaise
1 teaspoon seasoned salt
Pinch of garlic powder
1 heaped teaspoon freshly-
chopped chives*

1   Cook the macaroni according to the instructions on the packet. Drain and allow to cool.

2   Cut the ham into thin strips and add to the cooled macaroni. Add the cubed cheese, the grapes and the chopped celery.

3   Slice the ½ melon into thin slices and add to the salad. Shred the lettuce and add to the salad. Cover and keep cool while making the salad dressing.

4   To make the dressing, combine all the ingredients thoroughly in a bowl, and adjust the seasoning to taste. Just before serving, pour the dressing over the salad and toss well. Serve immediately.

Serving suggestion: For something a little extra special, try adding 100g/4oz of crumbled blue cheese to the salad dressing.

Roquefort Salad

The tarragon salad dressing is what makes this recipe very special.

Serves 8
Preparation time: 30 minutes

4 slices bacon, chopped
Vegetable oil, for frying
2 cloves garlic
4 slices bread, crusts removed
1 head endive
40g/1 ½oz Roquefort cheese
1 tablespoon freshly-chopped parsley

For the tarragon salad dressing:
1 tablespoon lemon juice
1 tablespoon freshly-chopped tarragon
Salt and freshly-ground black pepper
2 tablespoons vegetable oil
2 tablespoons olive oil

1   First prepare the salad dressing. In a bowl blend together the vinegar, lemon juice, tarragon and salt and pepper. Add both the oils slowly, whisking continuously.

2   In a frying pan, fry the chopped bacon until crisp. Drain on paper towels.

3   Pour enough oil into the frying pan to cover the garlic cloves. Halve the cloves and fry until the garlic begins to change colour, then remove from the oil.

4   Chop the bread slices into croûtons and fry in the hot oil until golden on all sides. Remove and drain on paper towels.

5   Wash and drain the endive. Tear up the leaves and place in a salad bowl. Crumble the cheese and add to the salad. Mix in the bacon and croûtons and the chopped parsley, and toss together well.

Serving suggestion: Just before serving, whisk the salad dressing and pour over the salad. Toss well and serve immediately.

Two-Cheese Courgette Bake

Serves 10
Preparation time: 25 minutes
Cooking time: 35 minutes

This baked luncheon dish also doubles up as a delicious appetiser.

100g/4oz butter
1 onion, chopped
2 cloves garlic, crushed
8 courgettes, sliced
225g/8oz Cheddar cheese, grated
75g/3oz freshly-grated Parmesan cheese

50g/2oz dry breadcrumbs
Salt and freshly-ground black pepper
1 teaspoon mixed dried herbs
3 eggs, beaten
125ml/4fl oz whipping cream

Pre-heat the oven to 180°C/350°F/Gas Mark 4

1 Lightly grease a glass baking dish.

2 In a large frying pan melt half the butter over a medium heat. Add the onion and garlic and cook for 4–5 minutes, stirring, until soft. Add the courgettes and continue to cook until tender, about 10 minutes. Remove the pan from the heat and add half the Cheddar cheese and half the Parmesan cheese. Season to taste and add the mixed herbs.

3 Spoon the mixture into the prepared baking dish. Sprinkle the remaining Cheddar over the top. In a small bowl combine the eggs and cream and pour over the courgettes. Sprinkle the remaining Parmesan over the top and dot with the remaining butter. Bake until golden-brown, about 35 minutes. Serve immediately.

Note: This dish can be prepared 1 day in advance if kept well wrapped in the refrigerator. Just reheat before serving.

Cheese and Fruit Sandwich

This very unusual grilled cheese sandwich also doubles up as a party appetiser if cut into small two-bite triangles.

Serves 2
Preparation time: 15 minutes
Cooking time: About 10 minutes

50g/2oz unsalted butter, softened
Pinch of salt
Pinch of freshly-grated nutmeg
Pinch of cinnamon
Pinch of ginger
Pinch of coriander
4 slices white bread, crusts removed
1 ripe pear, peeled and cored
2 slices Emmental cheese
2 slices Gruyère cheese

1 In a small bowl cream together the butter, salt, nutmeg, cinnamon, ginger and coriander. Spread this mixture on both sides of the bread.

2 Slice the pear lengthwise into four thick slices. Layer 1 slice of Emmental, 1 pear slice and 1 slice of Gruyère on 2 of the bread slices. Top each with a second bread slice and press down with the palm of your hand.

3 Heat a large frying pan and add the sandwiches. Weight the sandwiches down with a plate and cook until golden-brown, turning once. Serve immediately.

Serving suggestion: For something a little extra special, add 2 thin slices of ham to each sandwich.

California Salad

I suppose this isn't really a 'Californian' salad because I use a delicious cheese from Norway – Jarlsberg. Nevertheless, the combination of fruits and vegetables in this recipe will give you a taste of the West Coast.

Serves 6
Preparation time: 20 minutes

1 large bowl of assorted
 lettuce, (Iceberg, endive,
 cos, Webbs)
1 large bunch watercress
3 large oranges
2 grapefruit
1 ripe avocado
225g/8oz Jarlsberg cheese,
 cubed

For the salad dressing:
125ml/4fl oz vegetable oil
3 tablespoons red wine
 vinegar
½ teaspoon mustard
Pinch of sugar
1 clove garlic, crushed
2 tablespoons fine-chopped
 parsley

1 First prepare the salad dressing. Put all the dressing ingredients together in a screw-top jar, and shake them together thoroughly until well combined. Put aside.

2 Rinse the lettuce under cold water and allow to drain. Place in a large salad bowl, and add the watercress. Peel and slice the oranges, remove all the white pith and add to the salad bowl. Peel and section the grapefruit and peel and slice the avocado. Add both to the salad bowl, and then add the cubed cheese.

3 Just before serving, shake the salad dressing thoroughly and pour over the salad. Toss well to blend and serve.

Serving suggestion: You can, of course, try a wide variety of cheeses in this salad. Perhaps you have a favourite you'd rather use.

Main Dish Feta Salad

This colourful salad is ideal to serve at a barbecue or outdoor luncheon party.

Serves 4
Preparation time: 25 minutes

½ crisp lettuce, shredded
6–8 cherry tomatoes
¼ cucumber, peeled and chopped
50g/2oz Feta cheese, crumbled
½ red pepper, chopped
2 tablespoons finely-chopped chives
1 tablespoon margarine
50g/2oz chopped walnuts

For the dressing:
50ml/2fl oz olive oil
3 tablespoons lemon juice
2 tablespoons hazelnut oil
2 tablespoons raspberry vinegar
½ teaspoon mustard powder
¼ teaspoon dried thyme
Salt and freshly-ground black pepper

1 In a large bowl combine the lettuce, cherry tomatoes, cucumber, Feta cheese, chopped red pepper and chopped chives.

2 In a frying pan heat the margarine and add the walnuts. Stir fry the walnuts for 5 minutes and then add to the salad.

3 To make the dressing, combine all the ingredients together in a jar with a screw-top and shake well to combine. To serve, pour half of the dressing over the salad and toss well. Pass the remaining dressing around separately.

Serving suggestion: Either serve the salad in one large bowl or on individual plates.

Cheese Scones

Makes 6
Preparation time: 25 minutes
Cooking time: 15 minutes

These cheese scones are wonderful served with a salad luncheon.

200g/7oz plain flour
2 teaspoons sugar
2½ teaspoons baking powder
½ teaspoon salt
50g/2oz Cheddar cheese, grated

50g/2oz unsalted butter, chilled
2 eggs, beaten
70ml/2½fl oz whipping cream

Pre-heat the oven to 230°C/450°F/Gas Mark 8

1   Lightly grease and flour a baking tray.

2   In a large bowl sift together the flour, sugar, baking powder and salt. Add the cheese and butter and rub in until the mixture resembles fine breadcrumbs. Reserve 1 tablespoon of the beaten egg and add the remainder to the whipping cream in a small bowl. Then add to the dry ingredients and mix together with a fork.

3   Place the dough on a lightly-floured board and pat into a 20cm/8in circle. Cut into 6 equal wedges. Arrange the wedges on the prepared baking tray and brush with the reserved beaten egg. Bake until the scones are golden-brown, about 15 minutes. Serve hot or cold.

Note: These scones will keep very well for 1 week if kept in an airtight container.

3

Starters, Accompaniments and Soups

This chapter covers a whole range of cheese recipes to suit many different occasions. It includes starters to get your event off to a perfect beginning; accompaniments to complement both simple and exotic dishes; and wholesome, hot soups, which are delicious on their own with crusty bread, and can be served either as a light meal or as a starter.

Cheese demonstrates its tremendous versatility once again here in this chapter with delicious recipes using a variety of the most popular cheeses. I promise you, not only will you find recipes to fit your event, but you might also be tempted to organise an event around some recipe that takes your fancy! Go on . . .

Two-Cheese Biscuits

Makes about 24
Preparation time: 45 minutes
Cooking time: 15 minutes

Serve these cheese biscuits with soup or salads, or just pass them around at any time of day.

225g/8oz plain flour
1 teaspoon salt
2 teaspoons baking powder
½ teaspoon baking soda
½ teaspoon dry mustard
Pinch of cayenne pepper
2 tablespoons unsalted butter, chilled
100g/4oz Gruyère cheese, grated

About 175ml/6fl oz buttermilk
1 egg
1 egg yolk beaten with 1 tablespoon water, to glaze

For the topping:
2 tablespoons freshly-grated Parmesan cheese
2 tablespoons freshly-grated Gruyère cheese

Pre-heat the oven to 230°C/450°F/Gas Mark 8

1   Sift together the flour, salt, baking powder, baking soda, mustard and cayenne into a bowl. Add the butter and rub in until the mixture resembles fine breadcrumbs. Mix in the 100g/4oz grated cheese and make a well in the centre. Add 125ml/4fl oz of the buttermilk and the egg and blend together with a fork. Add additional buttermilk to make a sticky, workable dough.

2   Roll out the dough on a lightly-floured surface to about 2cm/¾in thick. Using a fluted biscuit cutter, cut out rounds and place on a lightly-buttered baking sheet. Brush the tops of the biscuits with the glaze.

3   For the topping, combine both the cheeses and sprinkle over the biscuits. Bake until golden brown, about 15 minutes. Serve hot.

Note: These biscuits freeze well for up to 1 month. Do reheat before serving because they really are at their best when they are hot.

Cheese Dip in Rye Bread

Here's a novel dish for guests to nibble at – great for everything from a barbecue to an outdoor luncheon party.

Serves 20
Preparation time: 20 minutes

1 round loaf of rye bread
225ml/8fl oz beer
75g/3oz mature Cheddar cheese, grated
75g/3oz Roquefort cheese, crumbled
½ teaspoon Worcestershire sauce
½ teaspoon tabasco sauce
½ onion, grated
2 garlic cloves, crushed
1 tablespoon butter, softened

1 Using a sharp knife, cut off the top of the loaf of bread and hollow out the centre. Scoop out the soft bread from the lid and break up the crusty top into bite-sized pieces (*see* note).

2 In a saucepan, heat through the beer then put aside to cool.

3 Place the beer in a blender or food processor with all the remaining ingredients. Blend until smooth.

4 Spoon the cheese mixture into the bread shell and surround with the bread pieces.

5 To serve, encourage your guests to dip into the cheese mixture with the bread pieces. When they're all gone, break off the sides of the bread shell to eat.

Note: Don't throw away the soft bread centre! Keep it for fresh or dry breadcrumbs.

Spinach Gratin

Serves 4
Preparation time: 30 minutes

A dish guaranteed to convert any vegetable hater.

675g/1½lb fresh, tender spinach
A little salt

For the cheese sauce:
2 tablespoons unsalted butter
2 tablespoons plain flour
350ml/12fl oz milk
Freshly-grated nutmeg

Salt and freshly-ground pepper
50ml/2fl oz whipping cream
2 teaspoons freshly-chopped tarragon
25g/1oz freshly-grated Parmesan cheese or 6 tablespoons grated mature Cheddar cheese or Gruyère cheese

1   First prepare the vegetables. Stem the spinach and rinse thoroughly. Place in a saucepan with very little water and a pinch or so of salt and cook until just tender. Drain and squeeze to remove all excess water and chop the spinach. Place in a gratin dish.

2   To make the cheese sauce, melt the butter in a saucepan over a low heat, add the flour and stir over the heat until foaming but not brown, about 2–3 minutes. Remove from the heat and very gradually add the milk, whisking continuously. Add some nutmeg and salt and pepper, then reduce the heat and cook for about 5 minutes, whisking constantly.

3   Whisk in the cream, bring to the boil, then reduce the heat and cook until the sauce thickens and coats the back of the spoon, about 7 minutes, whisking constantly. Remove from the heat, stir in the fresh tarragon and the grated cheese and adjust the seasoning if necessary.

4   Pour the sauce over the spinach, place under a hot grill and grill until bubbling and brown. Serve immediately.

Note: This cheese sauce can be prepared 1 day ahead if kept well covered in the refrigerator. Simply reheat before using.

Cheesey Dilled Potatoes

This is a wonderful accompaniment for any outdoor barbecue. Try cooking them on the grill – they're delicious.

Serves 8
Preparation time: 10 minutes
Cooking time: 1 hour

8 medium potatoes
6–8 green onions
1 teaspoon freshly-chopped dill (see note)

Salt and freshly-ground black pepper
2 tablespoons butter
175–225g/6–8oz Lancashire cheese, grated

Pre-heat the oven to 180°C/350°F/Gas Mark 4

1   Scrub the potatoes and pat dry with paper towels. Slice each potato very thinly but be careful not to cut all the way through.

2   Slice the green onions very thinly and sprinkle between the potato slices. Sprinkle the potatoes with the fresh dill and salt and pepper and top each with some butter.

3   Wrap in foil and bake until tender, about 50 minutes. Uncover the potatoes, sprinkle with the cheese and bake for a further 10 minutes, or until the cheese is melted and bubbling. Serve immediately.

Note: If fresh dill is not available, use ¼ teaspoon dry dill instead.

Pumpkin Soup

Serves 4
Preparation time: 30 minutes
Cooking time: 1 hour

As well as being delicious, this soup is such fun to serve in the pumpkin.

1 well-shaped pumpkin, about 2kg/5lb in weight
850ml/1½ pints chicken stock
275ml/½ pint whipping cream
Salt and freshly-ground black pepper

Freshly-grated nutmeg
500ml/2fl oz vegetable oil
3 slices white bread, crusts removed, and cut into cubes
100g/4oz Gruyère cheese, grated

1 Trim the base of the pumpkin so it will lie flat. Cut the top off to form a lid. Scrape out and remove the seeds.

2 Scoop out the flesh, leaving a 1cm/½in thick shell. Leave the shell and lid to one side.

3 Place the pumpkin flesh and stock in a large saucepan and bring to the boil. Reduce the heat and simmer until the liquid has reduced to about 450ml/16fl oz, about 30 minutes. Pour into a blender or food processor and purée. Add the cream, salt and pepper and nutmeg.

4 Heat the oil in a frying pan and fry the bread cubes until brown on all sides. Remove the croûtons with a slotted spoon and drain on paper towels.

Pre-heat the oven to 200°C/400°F/Gas Mark 6

5 Sprinkle half the cheese in the bottom of the pumpkin shell and top with half the croûtons. Spoon in the soup, sprinkle in the remaining cheese and top with the remaining croûtons. Place the lid on the pumpkin and bake in a shallow roasting tin until the pumpkin is tender, about 1 hour. Serve the soup from the pumpkin.

Serving suggestion: Stir the soup and serve immediately.

Cheese-Filled Bagels

It really is worth making all 52 of these delicious bagels because they freeze so well.

450g/1lb plain flour
225g/8oz vegetable lard,
* room temperature*
225ml/8fl oz iced water
1 egg
900g/2lb cottage cheese

225g/8oz cream cheese,
* room temperature*
1 egg
1 tablespoon sugar
½ teaspoon cinnamon
275g/10oz butter, melted

Makes 52
Preparation
time: 1 hour
(plus
refrigeration)
Cooking time:
45 minutes

1 Place the flour and lard in a bowl and rub together until the mixture resembles fine breadcrumbs. Stir in the iced water and egg, then knead to mix well. Divide the dough into 4 equal pieces and wrap in clingfilm. Refrigerate for at least 8 hours.

2 In a bowl beat together the cheeses, egg, sugar and cinnamon using an electric mixer.

Pre-heat the oven to 190°C/375°F/Gas Mark 5

3 Roll out one piece of the dough on a well-floured surface to a rectangle, measuring 45 × 65cm/18 × 26in and paper-thin. Spread one-quarter of the filling along the long side and roll up as for a Swiss roll. Cut into 5cm/2in pieces and place on a baking tray. Repeat with the remaining dough. Pour about 1 teaspoon of melted butter over each pastry and bake for about 45 minutes until golden-brown. Serve warm.

Note: The dough can be prepared up to 3 months ahead if kept well wrapped and frozen.

Swiss Cheese Custard

Serves 12
Preparation
time: 25
minutes
Cooking time:
35 minutes

This savoury custard is ideal to serve with cold meats and pâtés, accompanied with plenty of fresh, crusty bread.

50g/2oz butter
8 large leeks, the white
part thinly sliced
675g/1½lb Swiss chard,
trimmed and thinly
sliced
1 tablespoon lemon juice
3 tablespoons freshly-
chopped parsley

450g/1lb Gruyère cheese,
grated
6 eggs
700ml/1¼ pints single
cream
Salt and freshly-ground
white pepper
Pinch of freshly-grated
nutmeg

1 First melt the butter in a large saucepan. Over a medium heat cook the leeks for about 10 minutes, stirring occasionally until softened. Add the Swiss chard and the lemon juice and stir together for about 5 minutes. Mix in the parsley, remove from the heat and set aside.

Pre-heat the oven to 180°C/350°F/Gas Mark 4

2 Lightly butter a baking dish. Spoon the vegetable mixture into the baking dish and sprinkle with the cheese.

3 In a bowl beat together the eggs, cream, salt and pepper and nutmeg until well blended. Pour through a fine strainer over the vegetables. Bake for 15 minutes.

4 After 15 minutes, increase the oven temperature to 220°C/425°F/Gas Mark 7 and bake the custard until puffed and brown, about 20 minutes. Test by inserting a cake tester into the centre. If it comes out clean, the dish is ready.

Serving suggestion: Either serve the custard immediately while still hot or at room temperature.

Tomato Vinaigrette with Blue Cheese

Here's a wonderful side salad that's prepared in minutes. Choose to use whichever blue cheese you prefer.

Serves 6–8
Preparation time: 15 minutes

25g/1oz fresh parsley
1 tablespoon fresh tarragon
(see note)
1 garlic clove
125ml/4fl oz olive oil
50ml/2fl oz red wine vinegar

1 egg
Salt and freshly-ground black pepper
4 large, ripe but firm tomatoes
100g/4oz blue cheese

1 Place the parsley, tarragon and garlic in a blender or food processor and process until finely minced.

2 Add the oil, vinegar, egg, and salt and pepper and process for about 5 seconds.

3 Core the tomatoes and slice thinly. Arrange the slices on a serving dish and pour the dressing over the top. Crumble the blue cheese and sprinkle over the top of the salad. Serve immediately.

Note: If fresh tarragon is not available, use 1 teaspoon dried tarragon, crumbled, instead.

Chilled Consommé

**Serves 5
Preparation
time: 10
minutes (plus
refrigeration)**

This is one of those perfect soups that is delicious enough to serve at any dinner party, and yet is made from everyday ingredients you keep in the kitchen.

*175g/6oz Philadelphia
    cream cheese
1 tin consommé
1 tablespoon sherry*

*Salt and freshly-ground
    black pepper
Fresh parsley, to garnish*

1 Put the cream cheese, 12 tablespoons of the consommé, the sherry and salt and pepper to taste in a blender or food processor. Blend the ingredients together thoroughly.

2 Pour the mixture into 5 individual ramekin dishes, cover and store overnight in the refrigerator.

3 Pour equal amounts of the remaining consommé on top of the ramekins, cover once again and leave in the refrigerator to set.

Serving suggestion: Serve the consommé chilled from the refrigerator, garnished with fresh parsley.

Brie Soup

**Serves 4
Preparation
time: 25
minutes
Cooking time:
About 5
minutes**

I'm sure you'll love to share this baked soup with your friends.

*1 tablespoon butter
1 garlic clove, crushed
1 spring onion, sliced
50g/2oz mushrooms,
    chopped
850ml/1½ pints chicken
    stock*

*125ml/4fl oz whipping
    cream
Salt and freshly-ground
    white pepper
225g/8oz Brie cheese, cut
    into 8 pieces
8 thick slices French bread,
    toasted*

1   Melt the butter in a large saucepan and add the garlic, onion and mushrooms. Stir over a medium heat for 3 minutes.

2   Add the stock and bring to the boil. Gently boil the soup until the mixture reduces by one-third. Pour the soup through a fine strainer into another saucepan.

3   Add the cream and boil gently until slightly thickened. Season with salt and pepper.

Pre-heat the oven to 200°C/400°F/Gas Mark 6

4   Place one piece of cheese in the bottom of four individual heatproof soup bowls and ladle soup into each. Float one slice of French toast on top of each bowl and top each with one slice of the remaining cheese. Bake in the oven until bubbling – about 5 minutes. Serve immediately.

Serving suggestion: Instead of putting the soup in the oven to melt the cheese, you can use the grill. Keep a close eye on the cheese so it doesn't get overcooked.

Thick Vegetable Soup with Cheese Toast

Here's a wholesome soup for all the family to enjoy. It's quick and easy for those unexpected guests too.

Serves 6
Preparation time: 35 minutes

4 slices bacon
450g/1lb mixed vegetables (fresh or frozen), chopped (see note)
1.1 litres/2 pints beef stock
Salt and freshly-ground black pepper

6 slices French bread, toasted
175g/6oz Cheddar cheese, grated
Freshly-chopped parsley, to serve

1   First cook the bacon in a large saucepan for 3–4 minutes. Add the chopped vegetables and the beef stock. Bring to the boil, uncovered, and cook for about 10 minutes until the vegetables are tender.

2   Season the soup to taste with salt and pepper and ladle into 6 individual heatproof soup bowls. Float one slice of French toast on top of each and sprinkle with grated cheese.

3   Place the bowls of soup briefly under a hot grill just to melt the cheese. Sprinkle with the chopped parsley and serve immediately.

Note: Use any chopped vegetables you like for this soup, including carrots, cauliflower, broccoli and peas.

Creamy Stilton and Onion Soup

Serves 6–8
Preparation time: 20 minutes
Cooking time: 1 hour

This thick, rich and warming soup is ideal to make with any leftover Stilton you may have – especially around Christmas time.

50g/2oz butter
450g/1lb onions, sliced
1 clove garlic, crushed
350g/12oz potatoes, peeled and cubed
450ml/16fl oz milk
450ml/16fl oz water

Salt and freshly-ground black pepper
100g/4oz Stilton cheese, crumbled
Freshly-chopped parsley, to garnish

1   Melt the butter in a large saucepan, add the onion and garlic and cook, stirring occasionally, until softened – about 15 minutes. Do not allow to turn brown.

2   Add the cubed potatoes and stir in well with the onion. Add the milk and water, bring to the boil and season to taste with salt and pepper. Reduce the heat, partially cover and simmer for 1 hour.

3   Pour the soup into a blender or food processor and blend until smooth. Return to the saucepan, add the Stilton and stir over a low heat until the cheese has melted. Ladle the soup into individual soup bowls and serve immediately garnished with plenty of chopped parsley.

Serving suggestion: If you like, you can also serve this soup garnished with a swirl of whipping cream.

Cheese Loaf

Serves 20
Preparation time: 2 hours
Cooking time: 30 minutes

This 'bubble' loaf is perfect for a large luncheon or dinner party.

350ml/12fl oz milk
2 envelopes dry yeast
2 tablespoons sugar
3 tablespoons unsalted butter, melted
2½ teaspoons salt
About 525g/1lb 3oz plain flour (see recipe)

2 eggs
225g/8oz mature Cheddar cheese, grated
1 egg yolk beaten with 1 tablespoon water, to glaze
1 tablespoon sesame seed

1 Scald the milk in a small saucepan then pour into a large bowl and allow to cool slightly. Sprinkle the yeast and sugar over the milk, stir to dissolve and leave to stand for 15 minutes, until foamy. Stir in the melted butter and salt.

2 Beat about 225g/8oz of the flour into the yeast mixture using an electric hand mixer. Add the 2 eggs and cheese and beat until combined. Add a further 225g/8oz of the flour and beat until the dough is soft. Mix in just enough additional flour to make a firmer, manageable dough. Transfer to a floured surface and cover with a tea towel. Leave for 10 minutes.

3 Knead the dough on a lightly-floured surface until smooth. Butter a large bowl, place the dough in the bowl, cover with a tea towel and leave in a warm place for about 45 minutes, or until doubled in size.

4 Grease a baking tray. Knead the dough again until smooth, then roll into a log shape. Cut into 20 pieces and shape each piece into a ball. Place one ball in the centre of the baking tray and surround with the remaining balls so they are touching to form circles. Cover and leave to rise for 1 hour.

Pre-heat the oven to 180°C/350°F/Gas Mark 4

5   Brush the top of the loaf with the glaze and sprinkle with the sesame seeds. Bake for about 30 minutes or until the loaf sounds hollow when tapped on the bottom. Cool slightly before serving.

Note: This loaf freezes very well for up to 3 months.

Renee's No-Fail Cheese Soufflé

I promise you, this soufflé will *never* let you down. It's eminently versatile too. You can serve it as an accompaniment, a luncheon dish with salad, or as a starter.

Serves 6–8
Preparation time: 45 minutes (plus overnight refrigeration)
Cooking time: 1 hour

8 slices white bread, crusts removed
225g/8oz mature Cheddar cheese
6 large eggs
1 teaspoon salt
Pinch of cayenne
450ml/16fl oz milk
25g/1oz butter

1   Lightly butter a large soufflé dish. Cut the white bread into cubes. Grate the cheese.

2   In a bowl beat together the eggs, salt, cayenne and milk.

3   Alternate layers of bread, cheese and milk mixture in the prepared soufflé dish until all the ingredients are used up, ending with some cheese. Cover the dish with foil and refrigerate overnight.

Pre-heat the oven to 180°C/350°F/Gas Mark 4

4 Remove the soufflé from the refrigerator, un-cover and dot with the butter. Bake for 1 hour until golden-brown and lightly puffed.

Serving suggestion: This soufflé may be served hot or cold.

Cauliflower Cheese Soup

Serves 8
Preparation time: 30 minutes

This is a delicious cauliflower soup, but it's the swirl of basil cheese sauce that makes it extra special.

For the basil cheese sauce:
100g/4oz fresh basil leaves
2 garlic cloves
125ml/4fl oz olive oil
1 teaspoon salt
2 tablespoons walnuts
3 tablespoons mature Cheddar cheese, grated
3 tablespoons freshly-grated Parmesan cheese
3 tablespoons butter
Freshly-ground black pepper

For the soup:
1 cauliflower, cut into florets
1 potato, peeled and sliced
3 leeks, sliced
1.4 litres/2 pints 8fl oz chicken stock
Salt and freshly-ground black pepper

1 First make the basil cheese sauce. Put the basil, garlic, olive oil, salt and walnuts in a blender or food processor and purée. Transfer to a bowl and mix in the cheeses, butter and black pepper.

2 To make the soup, place the vegetables in a large saucepan with the stock and bring to the boil. Reduce the heat and simmer gently until all the vegetables are tender. Cool slightly.

3 Transfer the soup to a blender or food processor and purée. Season with salt and pepper.

4   To serve, reheat the soup gently and ladle into individual soup bowls. Swirl equal amounts of sauce into each bowl and serve immediately.

Note: This soup can be prepared up to 2 days ahead of serving. Cool completely and refrigerate.

Poppy Seed Cheese Loaf

A perfect bread to take on a picnic.

3 tablespoons poppy seeds
450g/1lb plain flour
2 tablespoons baking powder
1½ teaspoons salt
1 teaspoon baking soda

175g/6oz mature Cheddar cheese, grated
3 green onions, finely chopped
4 eggs
450ml/16fl oz buttermilk

Makes 3 loaves
Preparation time: 30 minutes
Cooking time: 35 minutes

1   In a small bowl pour boiling water over the poppy seeds and leave to soak until the seeds sink to the bottom – about 10 minutes. Drain and dry the seeds thoroughly on paper towels. Grease three loaf tins.

Pre-heat the oven to 190°C/375°F/Gas Mark 5

2   In a large bowl combine the flour, baking powder, salt and baking soda. Stir in the seeds, cheese and onion. Make a well in the centre, add the eggs, and whisk together until frothy. Whisk in the buttermilk and quickly mix in the flour. The batter should be lumpy.

3   Divide the mixture between the three loaf tins. Bake for about 35 minutes or until a cake tester inserted into the centre comes out clean.

Serving suggestion: Allow the loaves to cool to room temperature before serving.

Cream of Chilli Soup

Serves 8
Preparation time: 30 minutes

You can vary the quantity of chilli peppers used in this recipe depending on how much you like them!

3 tablespoons butter
3 tablespoons plain flour
450ml/16fl oz whipping cream
700ml/1 ¼ pints chicken stock
2 tablespoons butter
1 carrot, diced
1 onion, very finely chopped

1 green pepper, seeded and diced
3 chilli peppers, seeded and diced
100g/4oz Cheddar cheese, grated
100g/4oz Swiss cheese, grated
Salt

1 Melt the butter in a large saucepan over a low heat and add the flour. Stir for 3 minutes then mix in the cream and stock. Bring the mixture to the boil, stirring continuously, then reduce the heat and simmer gently until thickened – about 10 minutes.

2 Melt the 2 tablespoons butter in a small frying pan and add the carrot, onion and green pepper. Cook, stirring, for about 8 minutes, until soft. Add the chilli pepper and mix in.

3 Add both the cheeses and stir into the soup until melted. Add the vegetables and season to taste with salt.

Serving suggestion: Serve this soup immediately.

French Onion Soup

I love to start my dinner parties off with this soup.

Serves 4–6
Preparation time: 45 minutes

50g/2oz butter
225g/8oz onions, peeled and sliced
2 tablespoons flour
850ml/1½ pints rich, brown stock
Salt and freshly-ground black pepper
1 bay leaf
4–6 thick slices French bread
100g/4oz Gruyère cheese, grated

1 Melt the butter in a large saucepan and fry the onion until soft and just turning brown, about 5–10 minutes.

2 Spoon in the flour and mix well into the onion. Cook, stirring, for 1–2 minutes. Add the stock gradually and season with salt and pepper to taste. Add the bay leaf and bring to the boil. Cover and simmer for about 30 minutes.

3 Lightly toast the French bread slices on both sides.

4 To serve, ladle the soup into individual ovenproof soup bowls. Remove the bay leaf. Place one piece of French toast to float on each soup bowl, and sprinkle each with grated cheese. Place on a baking tray under a hot grill until the cheese has melted. Serve immediately.

Serving suggestion: Instead of using grated cheese, you can simply put a slice of cheese folded on top of each bread slice.

Savoury Edam

Makes about 425g/15oz
Preparation time: 20 minutes (plus setting aside time)

For the less formal get-together this cheese spread is a tasty and fun starter.

1.4–1.8kg/3–4lb whole
  Edam cheese 'ball'
225ml/8fl oz beer
50g/2oz butter, softened
1 teaspoon dry mustard

1 teaspoon carraway seeds
½ teaspoon seasoned salt
Melba toasts and crackers,
  to serve

1   Leave the cheese at room temperature for about 1 hour to soften.

2   Cut off the top of the cheese like a lid, and using a spoon, scoop out the cheese from the lid and from the cheese, keeping the shell intact. Discard the lid and refrigerate the shell.

3   Grate the scooped-out cheese into a bowl and leave until very soft. Add the beer, butter, mustard, carraway seeds and salt, and mix together until well blended. Spoon the mixture into the cheese shell, forming a high mound. Cover and refrigerate until ready to use.

4   To serve, leave at room temperature until the mixture is soft enough to spread. Serve with Melba toasts or a variety of crackers.

Note: If you wrap the cheese spread in clingfilm and then in foil, it will store in the refrigerator for several weeks.

4
Main Dishes

As we are so much more conscious of our health, our bodies, and our diet, what better time to incorporate cheese more completely into our meal planning? Cheese is an essential part of any diet for calcium, vitamin A, protein and therefore an important ingredient for delicious main dishes. Not only family meals, but more elaborate dinner party entrées are highlighted in this chapter. Have a flick through to find a whole range of exciting main dishes which will broaden your recipe repertoire.

Shrimp-Stuffed Edam

**Serves 2
Preparation
time: 25
minutes (plus
chilling)
Cooking time:
10–12 minutes**

A very glamorous meal for two. . . .

*Two 225g/8oz Edam
    cheeses
8 large shrimps, uncooked
2 tablespoons butter
25g/1oz finely-chopped
    onion
1 tomato, peeled and
    chopped
Salt and freshly-ground
    pepper*

*Pinch of cayenne
2 tablespoons freshly-
    chopped parsley
2 tablespoons fresh
    breadcrumbs
1 egg, beaten*

To garnish
*Cherry tomatoes, halved
Fresh parsley*

1 Peel away the wax from the cheeses. Cut across
   the top of each as for a lid and carefully scoop
   out the cheese from the centre, leaving a
   1½cm/¾in shell. Reserve the cheese and place
   the shells in iced water to chill for 1 hour.

2 Grate the cheese and place 50g/2oz in a bowl.
   Store the remaining cheese well wrapped in the
   refrigerator for future use.

3 Cook 2 of the shrimps in boiling salted water
   until just pink. Set aside for garnish. Peel and
   de-vein the remaining shrimps.

Pre-heat the oven to 180°C/350°F/Gas Mark 4

4 Grease two small baking dishes to fit each
   cheese shell. Melt the butter in a frying pan, add
   the onion and sauté until just golden. Add the
   remaining uncooked shrimps and sauté until
   just pink. Using a slotted spoon, add the onion
   and shrimps to the grated cheese, then add the
   tomato, salt and pepper and cayenne to the
   frying pan and simmer for 5 minutes until the
   liquid evaporates. Set aside to cool.

5 Add the tomato mixture to the grated cheese with the parsley, breadcrumbs and egg and mix together well. Adjust the seasoning to taste. Mound the mixture into the cheese shells and set in the prepared baking dishes. Bake until the cheese softens and just begins to melt, about 10 minutes – watch it very carefully! Serve immediately.

Serving suggestion: Serve garnished with the reserved shrimps, halved cherry tomatoes and fresh parsley.

3-Cheese Spinach Pasta Casserole

Here's a quick and easy entrée that is irresistible at large dinner parties.

**Serves 8
Preparation time: 35 minutes
Cooking time: 30 minutes**

1 tablespoon oil
A little salt
450g/1lb dried, corkscrew-shaped spinach pasta
225ml/8fl oz single cream
125ml/4fl oz white wine
Dash of tabasco sauce
450g/1lb blue cheese, crumbled
175g/6oz Brie cheese, finely chopped

100g/4oz mature Cheddar cheese, grated
1 tablespoon dry thyme
2 tablespoons dry sage
Freshly-ground black pepper
225g/8oz mature Cheddar cheese, grated
2 large tomatoes, sliced
Freshly-chopped parsley
Freshly-grated Parmesan cheese

Pre-heat the oven to 180°C/350°F/Gas Mark 4

1 Lightly butter a soufflé dish.

2 Place the oil in a large saucepan of boiling water, add the pasta and stir to prevent sticking. Cook until just tender, then drain and rinse under cold water. Drain thoroughly.

3   In a large saucepan combine together the cream, wine and tabasco over a low heat. Whisk in the blue cheese, the Brie and the 100g/4oz of Cheddar. Whisk until smooth then remove from the heat. Transfer about one-third of the pasta to the prepared dish and pour in one-third of the sauce. Sprinkle over about one-third of the remaining cheese. Repeat these layers two more times, ending with cheese.

4   Bake the casserole for 20 minutes, then cover the dish with foil and bake a further 15 minutes. Spread the tomato slices evenly over the top, sprinkle with parsley and then Parmesan cheese and bake a further 10 minutes, uncovered.

Serving suggestion: Serve this casserole with a large, crisp salad.

Full-of-Everything Pie

**Serves 10
Preparation time: 45 minutes (plus chilling)
Cooking time: 1 hour 20 minutes**

This is one of those wonderful deep pies filled with all kinds of goodies that everyone enjoys. Great for a big family get-together.

100g/4oz Swiss cheese, grated
100g/4oz mature Cheddar cheese, grated
1 pie crust, baked in a 25cm/10in springform tin
450g/1lb cooked crabmeat
100g/4oz cashews or walnuts
700ml/1¼ pints whipping cream

8 eggs, beaten
Salt and freshly-ground black pepper
2 tablespoons butter
¼ teaspoon dry tarragon
¼ teaspoon freshly-grated nutmeg
1 onion, very finely chopped
450g/1lb frozen, chopped spinach, thawed and thoroughly drained

Pre-heat the oven to 230°C/450°F/Gas Mark 8

1 Sprinkle both cheeses over the baked pie crust, then cover with the crabmeat and top with the nuts.

2 Mix together the cream and eggs, season with salt and pepper and pour half of this mixture into the pie crust. Reserve the remainder. Place the pie in the oven, reduce the heat to 180°C/350°F/Gas Mark 4 and bake for about 35 minutes, or until the custard has set.

3 Meanwhile, melt the butter in a large frying pan, stir in the tarragon, nutmeg and some pepper. Add the onion and stir over the heat until the onion is soft, about 10 minutes. Add the spinach and sauté for 3 minutes.

4 Reserve 50ml/2fl oz of the already reserved egg and cream mixture and blend the remainder into the spinach. Spoon on top of the pie and pour the reserved egg mixture over the top. Bake for a further 25–30 minutes or until the top is golden-brown. Leave to stand for about 30 minutes before serving.

Serving suggestion: Remove the springform tin and cut the pie into slices to serve.

Crispy Fish

You can use frozen fish instead of fresh for this recipe if you like.

700g/2lb fresh white fish fillets (such as cod or sole)
Salt and freshly-ground black pepper
6 tablespoons butter
1 onion, chopped

175g/6oz fresh breadcrumbs
100g/4oz mature Cheddar cheese, grated
1 teaspoon dry mustard
15g/½oz freshly-chopped parsley

Serves 6
Preparation time: 20 minutes
Cooking time: 20–25 minutes

Pre-heat the oven to 190°C/375°F/Gas Mark 5

1   Lightly grease a glass baking dish.

2   Season the fish with salt and pepper and arrange in the prepared dish.

3   Melt the butter in a frying pan, add the onion and stir for about 5 minutes until tender. Add all the remaining ingredients and mix together well.

4   Spread the mixture over the top of the fish fillets. Bake until the fish is cooked and flaky and the topping is golden-brown, about 20–25 minutes. Serve immediately.

Note: If you are planning ahead, this dish can be frozen for up to one month.

Veal Stuffed with Gorgonzola

**Serves 6
Preparation time: 20 minutes (plus marinating time)
Cooking time: 12 minutes**

A wonderful combination of flavours for a summer dinner party.

*6 veal loin chops, about 2.5cm/1in thick and 275g/10oz each
100g/4oz Gorgonzola cheese
2 tablespoons butter, softened
2 garlic cloves, cut in half
125ml/4fl oz white vermouth*

*125ml/4fl oz olive oil
4 spring onions, finely chopped
3 fresh sage leaves, crumbled
Salt and freshly-ground black pepper*

To garnish
6 fresh sage leaves

1   Using a sharp knife, cut a pocket horizontally through the centre of the muscle of each chop, but don't cut all the way through.

2 Cream together the cheese and butter. Spread this mixture evenly amongst the pockets, then close the pockets using a small skewer. Rub the cut side of the garlic all over the chops.

3 Combine together the vermouth, oil, spring onions, 3 fresh sage leaves and salt and pepper. Pour over the chops and leave to marinate for at least 1 hour, basting occasionally.

4 Pre-heat the grill. Pat dry the chops and grill until golden-brown, basting occasionally with the marinade. Don't overcook. Remove the skewers from the chops and arrange the chops on a serving dish. Garnish each one with a fresh sage leaf.

Serving suggestion: Serve this dish immediately with fresh vegetables.

Tortellini
with Blue Cheese Sauce

Serve this rich dish with plenty of fresh salad and French bread.

Serves 4
Preparation time: 50 minutes

6 large, dried Chinese mushrooms
2 tablespoons butter
3 tablespoons blue cheese, crumbled
3 tablespoons plain flour
1 tablespoon redcurrant jelly

350ml/12fl oz beef stock
450g/1lb fresh tortellini (see note), freshly cooked

To serve:
Freshly-grated Parmesan cheese

1 In a bowl, cover the mushrooms with warm water and leave to soften for about 30 minutes. Drain and squeeze the mushrooms dry, but reserve the juice. Discard the stems and chop the mushrooms.

2   Melt the butter in a saucepan and add the cheese. Stir with a wooden spoon until the cheese has melted. Don't worry if the mixture separates. Add the redcurrant jelly and stir until melted. Remove from the heat.

3   In a bowl combine the mushroom liquid and the stock and whisk into the cream mixture. Stir over the heat until the mixture thickens, about 5 minutes. Add the chopped mushrooms.

4   Place the freshly-cooked tortellini into a serving dish and pour the sauce over the top. Sprinkle with Parmesan cheese and serve immediately.

Note: I recommend you use fresh tortellini stuffed with chicken and/or veal, but of course you can choose whatever you prefer.

Mexican Chicken

Serves 8
Preparation time: 35 minutes (plus overnight refrigeration)
Cooking time: 20–25 minutes

You can choose to use either Gouda or Emmental cheese in this spicy recipe.

4 large chicken breasts, skinned, halved and boned
4 large canned green chillies
100g/4oz Emmental or Gouda cheese
50g/2oz dry breadcrumbs
25g/1oz Emmental cheese, grated
1 teaspoon chilli powder
¼ teaspoon garlic powder
Pinch freshly-ground black pepper

½ teaspoon ground cumin
6 tablespoons margarine, melted

For the spicy sauce:
2 × 225g/8oz cans tomato sauce
1 small green onion, chopped
½ teaspoon chilli powder
½ teaspoon ground cumin
Pinch of freshly-ground black pepper

1 Place the chicken breasts between pieces of greaseproof paper and, using a rolling pin, pound to a thickness of 5mm/¼in. Slice the chillies lengthwise and cut the cheese into 8 slices. Place one piece of chilli and one slice of cheese on each chicken breast and roll up to enclose the filling.

2 In a bowl combine the breadcrumbs, grated cheese, chilli powder, garlic powder, pepper and cumin. First dip the chicken in the melted margarine, then in the breadcrumb mixture. Place in a baking dish, seam side down and drizzle with any remaining melted margarine. Cover and refrigerate overnight.

Pre-heat the oven to 200°C/400°F/Gas Mark 6

3 Bake until the chicken is tender, about 20–25 minutes. Meanwhile, prepare the sauce.

4 Combine all the sauce ingredients in a saucepan and heat until hot, stirring, for about 5 minutes.

Serving suggestion: Serve the chicken immediately. Pass the sauce separately.

Chicken with Herb Cheese

Here's something a little bit different – stuffed chicken breasts with home-made herb cheese. This herb cheese is also very good served on its own with crackers.

Serves 4
Preparation time: 35 minutes (plus chilling)
Cooking time: 30 minutes

225g/8oz packet cream cheese, softened
1½ tablespoons whipping cream
50g/2oz butter, softened
¼ teaspoon garlic powder
Pinch of dry thyme
Pinch of dry oregano
Pinch of dry marjoram
Pinch of dry dill
Salt and freshly-ground pepper
4 whole chicken breasts, skinned and boned

1   Place all the ingredients except the chicken in a blender or food processor. Blend until just smooth. Place in a bowl, cover and chill for at least one hour (*see* note).

Pre-heat the oven to 180°C/350°F/Gas Mark 4

2   Pat the chicken breasts dry and lay between sheets of clingfilm. Using a rolling pin, flatten to about 5mm/¼in. Place 2 large tablespoons of the cheese mixture in the centre of each chicken breast, fold each chicken over and secure with cocktail sticks. Place in a baking dish and season with additional salt and pepper. Bake for about 30 minutes until springy to touch.

3   Drizzle any melted cheese in the baking dish over the chicken and serve immediately.

Note: The cheese stuffing can be prepared up to 1 week ahead if kept covered and stored in the refrigerator.

Goat Cheese Crêpes

Serves 4
Preparation time: 15 minutes
Cooking time: 10 minutes

Serve these unusual crêpes with your favourite home-made tomato sauce.

50g/2oz sifted plain flour
2 eggs, beaten
70ml/2½fl oz milk
70ml/2½fl oz water
1½ tablespoons vegetable oil
Pinch of salt

½ teaspoon mixed herbs
Melted butter
225g/8oz goat cheese

To serve:
Home-made tomato sauce

1   Place the flour, eggs, milk, water, oil, salt and herbs together in a bowl and combine well.

2   Heat a 15cm/6in frying pan over a medium heat and brush the bottom lightly with some of the melted butter. Add 2–3 tablespoons of the batter and tilt the pan to spread the batter evenly. Cook the crêpe until just done, then turn or flip and cook the other side until just done. Don't let the crêpe brown. Turn out on to a plate, keep warm and repeat with the remaining batter.

3   Spread about 2 tablespoons of the goat cheese down the middle third of each crêpe, then fold each crêpe over to enclose the filling. Transfer to a serving dish and serve immediately.

Serving suggestion: Either serve the crêpes with the tomato sauce ladled over, or pass the sauce around separately.

Hearty Vegetable Soup

Here's a wholesome soup, packed full of fresh vegetables, for all the family to enjoy.

Serves 6–8
Preparation time: 35 minutes

3 tablespoons butter
3 tablespoons plain flour
1 litre/1¾ pints chicken stock
275g/10oz broccoli, chopped
150g/5oz carrots, chopped
50g/2oz celery, chopped
1 small onion, chopped
1 garlic clove, crushed
Salt and freshly-ground black pepper
¼ teaspoon dry thyme, crumbled
225ml/8fl oz double cream
1 egg yolk
175g/6oz mature Cheddar cheese

1   Melt the butter in a large saucepan. Add the flour and stir for 2 minutes over a medium heat. Remove from the heat and gradually add the stock, stirring continuously. Bring the mixture to the boil, stirring.

2 Add the broccoli, carrots, celery, onion, garlic, salt and pepper and thyme, cover the pan and simmer for about 10 minutes or until the vegetables are tender.

3 Meanwhile, in a small bowl combine the cream and egg yolk. Gradually blend in a few tablespoons of the hot soup, then pour back into the soup and cook, stirring, until the soup thickens. Add the cheese and stir until the cheese has melted. Serve immediately.

Serving suggestion: Serve this soup with plenty of buttered toast or croûtons.

Feta Seafood Casserole

Serves 6
Preparation time: 30 minutes
Cooking time: 20 minutes

Serve this casserole over pasta or rice for a really hearty dish.

2 tablespoons olive oil
450g/1lb pickling onions, peeled
2 garlic cloves, crushed
1 large can chopped tomatoes
125ml/4fl oz white wine
1 teaspoon dry oregano
3 tablespoons freshly-chopped parsley

Salt and freshly-ground pepper
450g/1lb fresh fish (cod, haddock or halibut), cut into small pieces
100g/4oz uncooked prawns, peeled and de-veined
225g/8oz Feta cheese, cut into large chunks

1 Heat the oil in a large saucepan, add the onions and sauté until browned, about 5 minutes. Add the garlic and sauté gently, increase the heat and add the tomatoes, wine, oregano, half the parsley and salt and pepper. Bring the mixture to the boil, then reduce the heat, cover and simmer for about 10 minutes, stirring occasionally.

Pre-heat the oven to 200°C/400°F/Gas Mark 6

2   Spoon the tomato mixture into a large casserole
and top with the fish. Bake for 10 minutes,
covered, then add the prawns and sprinkle with
the Feta. Bake for a further 10 minutes until the
fish and prawns are cooked through. Sprinkle
with the remaining parsley and serve immediately.

Note: The tomato sauce can be prepared 1 day
ahead if kept covered in the refrigerator. Bring to
room temperature before using.

Beef and Potato Casserole

Here's a super hearty casserole to satisfy the
hungriest of families on a cold winter's evening.

Serves 4–6
**Preparation
time: 45
minutes
Cooking time:
10–15 minutes**

*1125g/2½lb potatoes,
  peeled
2 tablespoons butter
2 shallots, finely chopped
½ green pepper, chopped
2 garlic cloves, crushed
1 large tomato, chopped*

*350g/12oz minced beef
Salt and freshly-ground
  black pepper
1 bay leaf
50g/2oz Gruyère cheese,
  grated*

1   First boil the potatoes in plenty of salted water
until tender. Drain and mash. Butter a 20cm/8in
square baking tin.

Pre-heat the oven to 190°C/375°F/Gas Mark 5

2   Melt the butter in a large frying pan, add the
shallots and pepper and sauté for about 3
minutes. Increase the heat and add the garlic,
tomato, minced beef, salt and pepper and bay
leaf. Cook, stirring, until the beef is cooked,
about 10 minutes.

3   Spread about one-third of the mashed potato over the bottom of the prepared baking tin. Cover with half the beef mixture, then one-third of the potato and the remaining beef. Top with the remaining potato and sprinkle with the cheese. Bake for about 10–15 minutes or until the top is crusty and golden-brown.

Serving suggestion: Serve this casserole immediately with salad or freshly-cooked vegetables.

Eggs Mornay

Serves 8
Preparation time: 20 minutes
Cooking time: 20–30 minutes

This rich dish is ideal served either for brunch or supper.

4 eggs, hard-boiled
4 tablespoons butter
4 tablespoons flour
350ml/12fl oz milk
125ml/4fl oz double cream
Salt and freshly-ground black pepper

½ teaspoon freshly-grated nutmeg
75g/3oz Gruyère cheese, grated
25g/1oz freshly-grated Parmesan cheese

Pre-heat the oven to 230°C/450°F/Gas Mark 8

1   Lightly butter a 23cm/9in pie dish.

2   Cut each hard-boiled egg in half and arrange in the pie dish, cut side down.

3   Melt the butter in a saucepan, add the flour and stir over a low heat until the mixture falls away from the side of the pan. Add the milk slowly, stirring continuously over the heat until it begins to thicken. Add the cream, salt and pepper and the nutmeg, then add the Gruyère cheese and stir until the cheese has melted. The sauce will not be very thick.

4   Pour the cheese mixture over the eggs and sprinkle the top with the Parmesan cheese. Bake for 20–30 minutes or until golden-brown.

Serving suggestion: Serve immediately with plenty of boiled rice.

Shrimp Mornay with Peas

If you want to prepare this dish for a dinner party for 8, simply double all the ingredients, except the Worcestershire sauce. I suggest you use just 1½ teaspoons of this.

Serves 4
Preparation time: 40 minutes
Cooking time: 10 minutes

1½ tablespoons butter
1½ tablespoons flour
125ml/4fl oz milk
175ml/6fl oz double cream
Salt and freshly-ground pepper
Cayenne, to taste
75g/3oz Gruyère, Swiss or Cheddar cheese, grated

1 teaspoon Worcestershire sauce
75g/3oz frozen peas, thawed
450g/1lb shrimps or prawns, peeled, de-veined and cooked
25g/1oz freshly-grated Parmesan cheese

Pre-heat the oven to 200°C/400°F/Gas Mark 6

1   Melt the butter in a saucepan and stir in the flour using a wire whisk. Stir the mixture until smooth and just bubbling, then slowly add the milk and cream, stirring vigorously with the whisk. Simmer, stirring, for about 5 minutes.

2   Season with salt, pepper and cayenne to taste and remove from the heat. Stir in the cheese and Worcestershire sauce. If the mixture appears too thick, just thin with a little additional cream. Stir in the peas and shrimps or prawns and pour the mixture into a large casserole.

3   Sprinkle with the Parmesan cheese and bake for about 10 minutes, until hot, bubbling, and golden-brown.

Serving suggestion: Serve with plenty of boiled rice or noodles.

Spicy Stir-Fried Tofu

Serves 4–6
Preparation time: 20 minutes

Make sure you use the firm tofu (bean curd) for this recipe. You can find it in all good health food shops.

3–4 tablespoons sunflower oil (see *recipe*)
450g/1lb firm tofu, cut into 1cm/½in cubes
2 garlic cloves, crushed
¼ teaspoon cumin
¼ teaspoon dried thyme, crumbled
¼ teaspoon dried basil, crumbled

½ teaspoon curry powder
½ teaspoon dried dill, crumbled
¼ teaspoon dried turmeric
2 tablespoons soy sauce
50g/2oz freshly-grated Parmesan cheese

1   First heat the oil in a wok or large heavy-based frying pan over a high heat. Add the tofu and sauté for about 5 minutes, removing any excess water with a spoon.

2   Reduce the heat and add the garlic, cumin, thyme, basil, curry powder, dill and turmeric. Stir together well and add any additional oil necessary to prevent sticking.

3   Increase the heat and add the soy sauce and stir for 1 minute until heated through.

4   Using a slotted spoon, transfer the tofu to a serving dish and sprinkle with the cheese. Toss until the cheese melts and serve immediately.

Serving suggestion: Serve with boiled rice.

Cheese Fondue

A smooth, bubbling cheese fondue is always the making of a good, sociable evening.

Serves 4
Preparation
time: 15
minutes

1 garlic clove, cut in half
125ml/4fl oz dry white
   wine
1 teaspoon fresh lemon
   juice
275g/10oz Gruyère
   cheese, grated
275g/10oz Emmental
   cheese, grated

3 tablespoons kirsch
1 tablespoon cornflour
Pinch of nutmeg
Pinch of freshly-ground
   white pepper
Pinch of paprika
1 loaf French bread,
   cubed

1 Rub all over the inside of a fondue dish with the cut side of the garlic. Add the wine with the lemon juice and heat gently (*see* note).

2 Add both the cheeses gradually, stirring continuously until all the cheese is melted and combined.

3 In a small bowl blend together the kirsch and cornflour. Just as the cheese mixture begins to bubble, add the cornflour mixture. Continue to cook, stirring, for 2–3 minutes. Add the nutmeg, white pepper and paprika and adjust according to taste.

4 Place the fondue dish over the table burner and invite your guests to 'dig in' with the cubes of French bread on the end of long fondue forks.

Note: If you don't have a fondue dish, use a heavy-based saucepan.

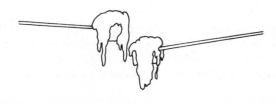

Gruyère Potatoes

Serves 8–10
Preparation time: 20 minutes
Cooking time: 35 minutes

This quick dish is so versatile you'll find it irresistible. It makes a wholesome luncheon meal or a very tasty accompaniment to another dish.

1125g/2½lb red new potatoes
350g/12oz Gruyère cheese, grated

Salt and freshly-ground black pepper
225ml/8fl oz single cream

1   First peel the potatoes, then boil for about 20 minutes until just tender. Drain thoroughly, slice thinly and put aside.

Pre-heat the oven to 180°C/350°F/Gas Mark 4

2   Lightly butter a baking dish. Layer half the potatoes in the bottom of the prepared dish. Sprinkle with half the cheese and some salt and pepper. Add the remaining potatoes, then pour over the single cream.

3   Top with the remaining cheese and a little more seasoning, and bake for about 35 minutes or until the potatoes are just browned and tender.

Serving suggestion: Serve immediately.

Cheddar Cheese Flan

Serves 8
Preparation time: 15 minutes
Cooking time: 20 minutes

You can find sun-dried tomatoes in good delicatessens. They really are worth the search, as their flavour is fantastic.

100g/4oz sun-dried tomatoes
450ml/16fl oz whipping cream

4 eggs
1 egg yolk
175g/6oz mature Cheddar cheese, grated

1   Place the tomatoes in a bowl and cover with water. Soak until just soft, drain thoroughly and chop.

Pre-heat the oven to 180°C/350°F/Gas Mark 4

2   Lightly butter 8 individual ramekins.

3   In a bowl beat together the cream, eggs and egg yolk. Add the cheese and tomatoes and beat together well. Divide evenly between the prepared ramekins and place in a fairly deep baking dish. Add boiling water to the baking dish to come half-way up the ramekins. Bake for about 20 minutes or until the flans are set. Serve immediately.

Serving suggestion: Serve the flans with a crisp, green salad.

Parmesan Chicken

It's the breadcrumb and Parmesan coating that keeps this chicken so succulent.

Serves 4
Preparation time: 20 minutes
Cooking time: 10 minutes

40g/1½oz freshly-grated Parmesan cheese
75g/3oz dry breadcrumbs
75g/3oz dry breadcrumbs
1 egg
4 chicken breasts, skinned and boned

Salt and freshly-ground black pepper
25g/1oz flour
3 tablespoons oil

To garnish:
1 lemon, cut into wedges

1   In a small bowl combine together the cheese and breadcrumbs. In another bowl whisk the egg with 1 tablespoon water.

2 Sprinkle the chicken breasts with salt and pepper and then dredge in the flour. Shake off any excess flour, then dip the chicken in the egg and coat with the breadcrumbs and cheese mixture (*see* note).

3 Heat the oil in a frying pan over a medium-high heat and cook the chicken, turning just once, until golden-brown – about 10 minutes. Serve immediately, garnished with lemon wedges.

Note: This recipe can be prepared up to this stage 2 hours before cooking. Just cover and keep in the refrigerator until ready to cook.

Pasta with Clam Sauce

Serves 6
Preparation time: 30 minutes

This dish is ideal for when you want to impress but don't have much time.

50g/2oz butter
50ml/2fl oz olive oil
1 green onion, finely
  chopped
225g/8oz jar clams
1 tomato, peeled and
  chopped
2 garlic cloves, crushed
½ teaspoon dry basil
½ teaspoon dry oregano

1½ teaspoons freshly-
  chopped parsley
Freshly-ground black
  pepper
450g/1lb fresh or frozen
  clams, chopped
450g/1lb freshly-cooked
  linguine *pasta*
50g/2oz freshly-grated
  Parmesan cheese

1 Melt the butter with the oil in a frying pan over a medium heat. Remove 2 tablespoons of the mixture and put aside. Add the green onion to the remaining butter and sauté for just 2 minutes. Drain the jar of clams and add the clam juice, tomato, garlic, basil, oregano and parsley to the onion. Season with salt and pepper and simmer for 10 minutes.

2   Add the clams from the jar and the fresh or frozen clams and continue to cook until heated through, about 3 minutes.

3   Add the reserved butter mixture to the freshly-cooked *linguine* and toss together in a large bowl. Add half of the Parmesan cheese and toss again. Toss with about half the clam mixture then top with the remaining.

Serving suggestion: Serve the *linguine* immediately, passing the remaining Parmesan around separately.

Quick Sausage and Egg Casserole

An excellent, wholesome dish when you're just too busy to cook.

225g/8oz French bread
900g/2lb sausage meat
16 eggs, beaten

175g/6oz mature Cheddar cheese, grated
Freshly-chopped chives

Serves 8
Preparation time: 30 minutes (plus overnight refrigeration)
Cooking time: 30–35 minutes

1   Lightly grease a large baking dish. Trim the crust from the French bread and cut into 2.5cm/1in cubes.

2   Arrange the bread cubes in the bottom of the prepared dish. Brown the sausage meat in a large frying pan, stirring and breaking up with the spoon, for about 15 minutes. Using a slotted spoon, sprinkle the sausage over the bread. Pour the eggs over the top, then sprinkle with the cheese and then the chives. Cover with foil and refrigerate overnight.

Pre-heat the oven to 180°C/350°F/Gas Mark 4

3   Uncover the dish and bake for about 30–35 minutes, until the eggs are set.

Serving suggestion: Allow the dish to cool for 5 minutes before serving.

Fettuccini Carbonara

Serves 4
Preparation
time: 30
minutes

This recipe is ideal for the 'slightly' weight-conscious pasta lover – the world-famous Fettuccini Carbonara without cream!

100g/4oz bacon
1 onion
3 eggs
50g/2oz freshly-grated
  Parmesan cheese

350g/12oz dry fettuccini
Salt and freshly-ground
  black pepper

1   First cook the bacon in a frying pan until golden-brown, about 10 minutes. Remove the bacon from the pan and drain on paper towels. Chop into pieces.

2   Chop the onion finely and place in the same frying pan. Cook the onion in the bacon fat over a medium heat until soft, about 5 minutes. Remove from the heat and put aside. Place the eggs in a bowl and beat well with the cheese.

3   Cook the pasta according to the instructions on the packet. Drain the pasta and return to the saucepan. Place over a low heat and add the bacon, onion, eggs and cheese and toss together until it is warmed through and the pasta is well coated. Season with salt and pepper and serve immediately.

Serving suggestion: Serve this delicious pasta dish with a large, crisp salad.

5

Vegetarian Specialities

Cheese as a nutritional food is an essential part of a vegetarian's diet. Of course, it can also play an important part in everyone's varied diet, but for vegetarians who have chosen to exclude meat from their diets, cheese can offer a valuable supply of protein.

In this chapter I have included recipes delicious enough for everyone. Gone are the days of vegetarians having to live on bland, boring diets. Today we are all much more aware of the health value of diets without meat, or with less meat, and so the value of healthy alternatives such as cheese has become more significant. Vegetarian or non-vegetarian, I hope you will try the recipes in this chapter and enjoy them.

Sage and Onion
Bread Pudding

Serves 8
Preparation
time: 1 hour
Cooking time:
1 hour

This savoury pudding served hot from the oven is delicious, but don't bother reheating any leftovers – they're great just served at room temperature.

2 tablespoons butter
1 large garlic clove,
*   crushed*
3 red onions, finely sliced
2 leeks, white part only
*   sliced*
150g/5oz Münster cheese,
*   grated*
2 teaspoons finely-chopped
*   fresh sage*

400ml/14fl oz milk
3 eggs
Salt and freshly-ground
*   black pepper*
2 teaspoons mustard
175g/6oz wholewheat
*   bread, crusts removed*
*   and cut into cubes*

1   Melt the butter in a large frying pan, add the garlic, onion and leeks. Cover and cook gently for about 12 minutes, then remove the cover and continue to cook until all the liquid has evaporated. Stir occasionally for about 8 minutes.

2   In a large bowl mix together the cheese and sage. Add 175ml/6fl oz of the milk, the eggs, salt and pepper and mustard and beat together well (*see* note). Stir in the remaining milk.

3   Place the bread cubes in a buttered baking dish. Pour the egg mixture over the bread and, using a fork, distribute the onion evenly through the bread. Put aside for 30 minutes to soak. The pudding can be prepared up to this stage 12 hours ahead. Keep it covered in the refrigerator, but bring back to room temperature before cooking.

Pre-heat the oven to 150°C/300°F/Gas Mark 2

4 Bake the pudding for 45 minutes then increase the oven temperature to 230°C/450°F/Gas Mark 8 and bake a further 15 minutes until browned and puffy. Allow to stand for 15 minutes before serving.

Note: To get these ingredients thoroughly combined, try blending them in a blender or food processor. Then stir in the remaining milk and continue as for the recipe.

Fried Aubergine with Goat Cheese

I have chosen to use firm Feta cheese in this recipe, but you can choose whichever goat cheese you prefer.

Serves 8
Preparation time: 35 minutes (plus chilling)
Cooking time: 35–40 minutes

8 aubergines, cut into 1cm/½in slices
Salt, to sprinkle
175ml/6fl oz olive oil
4 ripe tomatoes, peeled and mashed
4 garlic cloves, crushed
2 teaspoons dried oregano, crumbled
100g/4oz Romano cheese, grated
225g/8oz Feta cheese, crumbled
50ml/2fl oz milk
1 egg
Salt and freshly-ground black pepper

1 Lay the slices of aubergine on a plate and sprinkle with salt. Leave to stand for 15 minutes, then rinse off the salt and pat dry.

2 Heat the oil in a large frying pan and add the aubergine in batches. Fry until golden on both sides (you may need to add extra oil), then transfer to paper towels and drain.

Pre-heat the oven to 180°C/350°F/Gas Mark 4

3   Make a single layer of aubergine at the base of a baking dish. Combine the tomatoes, garlic and oregano and pour about one-third of this mixture over the aubergine. Top with one-third of the Romano and one-third of the Feta cheese. Repeat 2 more layers of each.

4   In a small bowl beat together the milk and egg. Season to taste and pour over the top. Bake for 35–40 minutes or until the aubergine is golden-brown. Serve immediately.

Note: This dish can be prepared 1 day ahead. Simply reheat in the oven at the same temperature for about 10 minutes.

Goat Cheese and Leek Flan

Serves 6
Preparation time: 30 minutes
Cooking time: 30 minutes

Leeks and goat cheese make the perfect combination. Serve this flan either as a starter or luncheon dish.

1 prepared 25cm/10in pie crust
4 tablespoons butter
6 leeks, white part only, sliced
About 4 tablespoons water
Salt and freshly-ground pepper

2 eggs
125ml/4fl oz single cream
4 tablespoons butter, softened
225g/8oz goat cheese
½ teaspoon freshly-chopped thyme

1   First prepare your favourite pie crust. Set aside.

2   Melt the butter in a frying pan, add the leeks and sauté for about 20 minutes. Add the water and salt and pepper to taste.

3   Place all the remaining ingredients in a blender or food processor and blend until smooth.

Pre-heat the oven to 200°C/400°F/Gas Mark 6

4 Spread the leeks in the prepared pie crust and pour the cheese mixture over them. Bake for about 30 minutes or until the flan is set and the top golden-brown.

Serving suggestion: This flan can be served hot or cold.

Goat Cheese Sandwich

I have suggested you use French or Italian bread for this recipe, but you can of course choose another variety if you wish.

Serves 6–8
Preparation time: 35 minutes

25g/1oz red onion
225g/8oz soft goat cheese, cut in four
6 sun-dried tomatoes, soaked and drained
2 teaspoons freshly-chopped oregano
2 large Italian tomatoes, cored
1 large loaf French or Italian bread
12 large, tender spinach leaves
12 large radicchio leaves

1 Place the onion, cheese, sun-dried tomatoes and oregano in a blender or food processor and blend until smooth. Transfer to a bowl (*see* note).

2 Slice the tomatoes thinly. Halve the bread lengthwise and hollow out the loaf leaving a 1cm/½in shell. Spread the cheese mixture evenly in both halves. Place the tomato slices in the bottom half and top with the spinach and radicchio leaves. Cover with the top half of the bread and press together lightly.

3 To serve, cut the loaf diagonally into slices and arrange on a serving dish, cut side up. Serve immediately.

Note: This filling can be prepared 1 day ahead. Cover well and refrigerate until ready to use.

Broccoli and Egg Casserole

Serves 6
Preparation time: 35 minutes
Cooking time: 25 minutes

Here's a wholesome vegetarian dish that is ideal for the busy cook.

450g/1lb fresh broccoli, trimmed and sliced
100g/4oz unsalted butter or margarine
2 tablespoons finely-chopped onion
25g/1oz plain flour
½ teaspoon dry mustard
575ml/1 pint milk

100g/4oz mature Cheddar cheese, grated
Salt and freshly-ground black pepper
75g/3oz fresh wholemeal breadcrumbs
6 hard-boiled eggs, cut in half

1   Cook the broccoli in a little boiling water for about 15 minutes or until tender. Drain well.

2   In a small saucepan melt half the butter or margarine and sauté the onion for about 3 minutes. Add the flour and mustard and cook for 1 minute, stirring. Add the milk slowly, stirring continuously, and stir over the heat until thickened and bubbly, about 5 minutes. Add the cheese and stir until melted, then add salt and pepper to taste. Set aside.

Pre-heat the oven to 180°C/350°F/Gas Mark 4

3   Lightly butter a baking dish. Melt the remaining butter or margarine in a small saucepan, add the breadcrumbs and stir until crisp and golden.

4   Arrange the broccoli in the bottom of the prepared dish and top with the hard-boiled eggs. Pour the cheese sauce over the top and sprinkle with the crisp breadcrumbs. Bake for about 25 minutes or until heated through. Serve immediately.

Serving suggestion: Serve this dish with a crisp, green salad.

Individual Goat Cheese Tarts

These tarts make a quick yet elegant appetiser.

Prepared puff pastry, cut into four 13 × 13cm/ 5 × 5in squares
2 tablespoons prepared pesto sauce (see note)
2 tablespoons goat cheese

1 courgette, cut into slices
1 tomato, cut into 12 wedges
Freshly-grated Parmesan cheese
Olive oil, to drizzle

Makes 4
Preparation time: 20 minutes
Cooking time: 30 minutes

Pre-heat the oven to 200°C/400°F/Gas Mark 6

1 Fold each square up around the edges to form a tart case.

2 In a small bowl blend together the pesto sauce and goat cheese. Divide between the tart cases and spread out in each. Arrange the courgette and tomato slices evenly over the top and sprinkle with Parmesan cheese and a little olive oil.

3 Place the tarts on a baking tray and bake for about 30 minutes or until the courgette is tender and the pastry is golden-brown around the edge. Serve immediately.

Note: You can find ready-made pesto sauce in most good supermarkets.

Mangetout Fettuccini

Serves 6–8
Preparation
time: 30
minutes

This fresh-tasting, colourful combination makes an excellent luncheon dish, starter or accompaniment.

1 tablespoon butter
1 garlic clove, crushed
2 shallots, finely chopped
225ml/8fl oz white wine
450ml/16fl oz whipping
    cream
1 tablespoon freshly-
    chopped tarragon
100g/4oz mangetout,
    trimmed and cut in half
    horizontally
1 large tomato, diced
Salt and freshly-ground
    black pepper

50g/2oz freshly-grated
    Parmesan cheese
225g/8oz freshly-cooked
    green fettuccini
225g/8oz freshly-cooked
    white fettuccini
Freshly-grated Parmesan
    cheese

To garnish
Finely-chopped spring
    onions
Tarragon sprigs

1   Melt the butter in a wok or large, heavy-based frying pan, add the garlic and shallots and sauté until soft. Add the wine and simmer for about 5 minutes, until the mixture is reduced to 2 table-spoons. Add the cream and tarragon and simmer for about 10 minutes, until the mixture is reduced to about 350ml/12fl oz.

2   Stir in the mangetout and tomato and heat through. Stir in half the Parmesan cheese and salt and pepper to taste.

3   In a large serving bowl, combine the fettuccini. Pour the sauce over the top and toss. Sprinkle with the remaining cheese.

Serving suggestion: Serve immediately garnished with chopped spring onions and fresh tarragon sprigs.

Swiss Cheese Bake

This is the perfect family dish to make if you're in a hurry.

Serves 4
Preparation time: 25 minutes
Cooking time: 40 minutes

*3 thick slices wholemeal
   bread, crusts removed*
*About 2 tablespoons
   vegetable oil*
3 tomatoes, sliced
*225g/8oz Gruyère or
   Emmental cheese, grated*

350ml/12fl oz milk
2 eggs
*Salt and freshly-ground
   black pepper*
Pinch of paprika
Pinch of dry mustard

1   Cut the bread into cubes. Heat the oil in a frying pan and fry the bread cubes until crisp and golden on both sides.

2   Lightly grease a pie dish and arrange the croûtons in the dish. Layer the tomatoes on top and sprinkle evenly with the cheese.

Pre-heat the oven to 180°C/350°F/Gas Mark 4

3   In a bowl beat together the milk, eggs, salt and pepper, paprika and mustard. Pour over the cheese and bake for 40 minutes until browned. Serve immediately.

Serving suggestion: Serve with boiled potatoes and a crisp salad.

Multi Cheese-Stuffed Peppers

Serves 8
Preparation time: 20 minutes
Cooking time: 20 minutes

This recipe, combining the flavours of four different cheeses, makes an excellent appetiser.

4 small red peppers, halved and seeded, stems remaining
4 small green peppers, halved and seeded, stems remaining
100g/4oz Feta cheese, crumbled
175g/6oz Ricotta cheese, drained
225g/8oz Mozzarella cheese, grated

5 tablespoons freshly-grated Parmesan cheese
15g/½oz freshly-chopped parsley
1 tablespoon capers, finely chopped
25g/1oz finely-chopped onion
1½ teaspoons freshly-ground black pepper
1½ teaspoons dried oregano, crumbled
8 small, crisp lettuce leaves

1 First place the peppers under a hot grill and char until blackened but firm. Put aside to cool, then peel.

Pre-heat the oven to 200°C/400°F/Gas Mark 6

2 In a large bowl combine all the remaining ingredients except the lettuce. Mound the mixture into the peppers and arrange in a baking dish. Heat through in the oven for about 20 minutes.

Serving suggestion: Line a serving dish with the lettuce leaves and place the peppers on top. Serve immediately.

Farmhouse Omelette

Here's a hardy omelette that's made special when served with soured cream.

50g/2oz butter
1 onion, thinly sliced
2 medium boiling potatoes, peeled and diced
½ teaspoon dried dill
2 tablespoons freshly-chopped chives
6 eggs
125ml/4fl oz milk

Salt and freshly-ground black pepper
100g/4oz mature Cheddar cheese, grated
1 tomato, peeled and sliced
1 green pepper, thinly sliced into rings
225ml/8fl oz soured cream, to serve

Serves 4
Preparation time: 25 minutes
Cooking time: 20 minutes

1   Melt the butter in a 25cm/10in frying or omelette pan, add the onion and potato and sauté until tender, stirring, for about 20–25 minutes. Add the dill and chives.

2   In a bowl whisk together the eggs, milk and salt and pepper until well blended. Pour over the onion mixture, reduce the heat to 'low' and cook, covered, for 15–20 minutes until set. Be careful not to overcook.

3   Pre-heat the grill. Sprinkle the top of the omelette with half the cheese, then arrange the tomato and pepper on top. Sprinkle with the remaining cheese and place under the grill until the cheese melts.

Serving suggestion: Serve the omelette immediately with the soured cream.

Baked Macaroni Cheese

Serves 4–6
Preparation time: 20 minutes
Cooking time: 15–20 minutes

Children love this creamy macaroni cheese. You can serve it either as a main course or as an accompaniment.

225g/8oz macaroni
50g/2oz butter
25g/1oz plain flour
1 teaspoon salt
Pinch of freshly-ground pepper

450ml/16fl oz creamy milk
225g/8oz mature Cheddar cheese, grated

Pre-heat the oven to 190°C/375°F/Gas Mark 5

1 Cook the macaroni according to the instructions on the packet. Drain.

2 Melt the butter in a saucepan, remove from the heat and add the flour, salt and pepper. Stir together until smooth then slowly add the milk. Replace on the heat and bring to the boil, stirring continuously. Reduce the heat and simmer gently for 1 minute. Remove from the heat.

3 Add three-quarters of the cheese and the macaroni to the sauce and pour the mixture into a casserole dish. Sprinkle over the remaining cheese. Bake for about 15–20 minutes, or until golden-brown. Serve immediately.

Serving suggestion: Macaroni cheese can be very versatile. Try adding chopped ham, cooked vegetables or prawns to the above recipe for something a little different.

Blue Cheese Potato Salad

This side dish is a sensation for any barbecue.

Serves 8
Preparation time: 35 minutes

For the dressing:
50ml/2fl oz cider vinegar
2 tablespoons herb vinegar
175ml/6fl oz olive oil
2 tablespoons freshly-chopped parsley
25g/1oz finely-chopped shallots
2 teaspoons mustard
Salt and freshly-ground black pepper

For the salad:
1.8kg/4lb new potatoes, unpeeled
Lettuce leaves
1 bunch watercress
125ml/4fl oz whipping cream
75g/3oz blue cheese
3 tablespoons freshly-chopped chives

1   First make the dressing. In a small bowl mix together the vinegars, oil, parsley, shallots and mustard. Whisk in the salt and pepper and set aside.

2   To make the salad, boil the potatoes until just tender. Allow to cool slightly then slice. Place in a bowl and gently stir in about 125ml/4fl oz of the dressing.

3   Line a large serving platter with the lettuce leaves. Top with alternate rows of potato and watercress. Beat the cream and cheese into the remaining dressing and spoon over the potatoes. Sprinkle the chives over the top and serve.

Serving suggestion: This salad can be served hot or at room temperature.

Cheddar-Stuffed Potato Skins

Serves 4
Preparation time: 20 minutes
Cooking time: 15 minutes

This delicious recipe can be served either as an appetiser or as a luncheon dish.

4 medium baking potatoes, baked and cooled
225g/8oz mature Cheddar cheese, grated
2 egg whites
50g/2oz jar pimentos, finely chopped
2 green onions, finely chopped

50g/1oz fresh breadcrumbs
Vegetable oil, for deep frying

To serve:
Soured cream
Freshly-chopped chives

1   First cut the baked potatoes horizontally and scoop out the pulp leaving a 5mm/¼in shell. Reserve the pulp for another use and put the shells aside.

2   In a small bowl mix together the cheese, egg whites, pimentos and onion until well combined. Divide between the potato shells, forming a mound on the top. Sprinkle with the breadcrumbs to cover completely.

Pre-heat the oven to 180°C/350°F/Gas Mark 4

3   Heat the oil in a deep-frying pan to 180°C/350°F. Fry the potatoes in the oil for about 50 seconds until the breadcrumbs are golden. Drain on paper towels.

4   Arrange the potatoes on a baking tray and bake in the oven for about 15 minutes or until the cheese is melted.

Serving suggestion: Serve the potatoes immediately with plenty of soured cream and freshly-chopped chives.

Chèvre
and Green Bean Salad

Here's a salad typical of southern France. It makes a lovely appetiser or light luncheon dish.

Serves 4
Preparation time: 50 minutes

2 tablespoons red wine
  vinegar
1 small onion, very finely
  chopped
400g/14oz very thin French
  green beans, trimmed
10 fresh mint leaves,
  chopped
14 fresh basil leaves,
  chopped

4 large tomatoes, sliced
100g/4oz Chèvre cheese,
  cut into about 20 slices
8 black olives, pitted and
  chopped
Salt and freshly-ground
  black pepper
Olive oil and red wine
  vinegar, to drizzle

1   In a small bowl mix together the vinegar and onion and set aside for 30 minutes. Steam the green beans until just tender but still crisp. Rinse under cold water and drain.

2   Drain the onion and return to the bowl. Combine the mint and basil and add all but 2 tablespoons to the onion.

3   Arrange half the tomato slices on a serving dish, top with half the Chèvre slices and sprinkle with half the onion mixture. Repeat these layers. Arrange the green beans around the edge of the serving dish and sprinkle all over with the reserved mint and basil. Sprinkle the olives over the beans and season the salad with salt and pepper (*see* note).

4   Just before serving, sprinkle a little olive oil and red wine vinegar over the salad.

Note: The salad can be prepared to this stage 1 hour ahead. Keep covered tightly and at room temperature until ready to use.

Rainbow Pasta

Serves 4
Preparation
time: 40
minutes

This colourful dish filled with crisp, fresh vegetables is wonderful to serve at a luncheon party.

225g/8oz wholewheat
pasta shells
225g/8oz tri-coloured
spiral pasta
2 large carrots, peeled and
thinly sliced
75g/3oz broccoli florets

50g/2oz pitted black
olives, sliced
450ml/16fl oz whipping
cream
50g/2oz freshly-grated
Parmesan cheese
Salt and freshly-ground
black pepper

1   First cook the pasta according to the instructions on the packet. Drain, place in a bowl and keep warm.

2   Steam the carrots and broccoli until just tender but still crisp. Place in a bowl with the pasta, add the olives and keep warm.

3   In a small saucepan combine the cream, cheese and salt and pepper. Stir over a medium heat until slightly thickened, about 8 minutes. Pour over the pasta, toss to coat completely and transfer to a serving dish. Serve immediately.

Note: You really can include any of your favourite vegetables in this recipe. The more colours the better!

6
Low-Calorie Dishes

You know, diets really don't have to be boring at all! Here is a chapter filled with low-calorie dishes, all wholesome and delicious and all with the added beauty of cheese. It is so important when trying to lose weight to eat nutritionally-balanced meals as well as to keep the calories down. Because of its nutritional value, cheese can be a very important part of your calorie-reduced plan. I'm sure you will enjoy these recipes and forget you're on a diet . . . in fact, serve some to your guests and family and see what they have to say!

Cheddar Cheese Chips

**Makes 16
Cooking time:
10 minutes
Calories per
chip: 10 (40
kilojoules)**

Cheese and only cheese, these chips are ideal served with soup or salad or as a party appetiser.

*100g/4oz mature Cheddar
cheese*

Pre-heat the oven to 150°C/300°F/Gas Mark 2

1   Cut the cheese into 16 cubes. Place on a baking tray lined with greaseproof paper as far apart as possible as they will spread.

2   Bake the cheese until it melts into thin discs and the edges brown, about 10 minutes.

3   Using a spatula, transfer to drain on paper towels and blot to remove any excess oil.

Serving suggestion: Serve these chips warm or at room temperature.

Sole Stuffed with Shrimp and Feta Cheese

**Serves 6
Preparation
time: 30
minutes
Cooking time:
30 minutes
Calories per
serving: 199
(837 kilojoules)**

Serve this light entrée at any dinner party – it's so attractive and delicious, no one would ever know it is so low in calories!

*175g/6oz cooked shrimps
   or prawns
175g/6oz Feta cheese
2 tablespoons water
3 spring onions, green
   parts only chopped
6 water chestnuts, chopped*

*100g/4oz finely-chopped,
   tender fresh spinach
6 × 100g/4oz fillets of sole
Salt and freshly-ground
   black pepper
50ml/2fl oz white wine
6 thick tomato slices
6 watercress leaves*

1   Set aside 3 of the shrimps or prawns and chop the rest into a bowl. Crumble the cheese into the bowl, mix in the water, then add three-quarters of the onion, water chestnuts and spinach.

Pre-heat the oven to 170°C/325°F/Gas Mark 3

2   Pat the fish dry and lay it on a work surface. Sprinkle with a little pepper and spread even amounts of shrimp or prawn mixture on each fillet. Roll each fillet up from the short end and secure with cocktail sticks. Arrange in a baking dish, pour over the wine and bake for 15–20 minutes or until the fish is cooked.

3   While the fish is cooking, arrange the tomato slices on a baking dish and sprinkle with a little salt and pepper. Place a watercress leaf on top of each and bake for 15 minutes.

Serving suggestion: Transfer the sole and baked tomato slices to individual plates. Top each sole with half a reserved shrimp or prawn and sprinkle with the remaining onion. Serve immediately.

Artichoke Flan

Here's a flan with no pastry – that's what makes it deliciously low in calories.

Juice and rind of 1½ lemons
12 small artichokes
3 tablespoons olive oil
1 garlic clove
125ml/4fl oz water

6 eggs
50ml/2fl oz water
Salt and freshly-ground black pepper
50g/2oz mature Cheddar cheese, grated

Serves 6
Preparation time: 40 minutes
Cooking time: 15 minutes
Calories per serving: 220 (921 kilojoules)

1   First fill a bowl with water and add the juice and rind of ½ lemon.

2 To prepare each artichoke, first cut off the stems and rub with ½ lemon. Carefully break off and discard the outer leaves leaving a cone of centre leaves. Cut off about 1cm/½in off the top of the cones. Trim the hearts and remove any dark green areas. Halve each artichoke lengthwise, rub with lemon and place in the bowl of water.

Pre-heat the oven to 180°C/350°F/Gas Mark 4

3 Heat the oil in a large frying pan, add the unpeeled garlic and cook for 2 minutes. Drain the artichokes, slice each lengthwise and sprinkle with the remaining lemon. Add to the garlic with the 125ml/4fl oz water, cover and simmer until tender, about 15 minutes.

4 Lightly butter a baking dish, drain the artichokes and arrange in the dish. In a bowl combine the eggs, 50ml/2fl oz water and salt and pepper. Pour over the artichokes and sprinkle with the cheese. Bake until the eggs are cooked, about 15 minutes.

Serving suggestion: Serve the flans immediately from the oven.

Summer Plate

**Serves 4
Preparation
time: 20
minutes
Calories per
serving: 275
(115 kilojoules)**

The perfect dish for a summer luncheon.

*1 crisp lettuce
50g/2oz Edam cheese,
grated
350g/12oz cottage cheese
Salt and freshly-ground
black pepper*

*Pinch of paprika
100g/4oz ham, chopped
225g/8oz seedless
grapes
4 ripe peaches, stoned*

1 First wash and drain the lettuce. Arrange the lettuce on a large serving dish.

2 In a bowl mix together the Edam and cottage cheese, salt and pepper to taste, paprika and the ham. Combine together well then make a heap of this mixture in the middle of the lettuce.

3 Thoroughly wash the grapes. Slice the peaches into quarters. Arrange the grapes and peaches around the cheese mixture and serve at once.

Serving suggestion: This cottage cheese mixture also makes an ideal low-calorie dip. Try it for your next party but double the quantities given here.

Surprise Hamburgers

These tasty hamburgers with cheese topping can also be prepared on the barbecue.

Serves 4
Preparation time: 30 minutes
Cooking time: 15 minutes
Calories per serving: 290 (1214 kilojoules)

For the burgers:
350g/12oz minced beef
1 onion, finely chopped
1 stock cube
Salt and freshly-ground black pepper
1 teaspoon mixed herbs
1 egg

For the topping:
1 tablespoon vegetable oil
50g/2oz mushrooms, sliced
1 teaspoon horseradish sauce
50g/2oz Edam cheese, grated

To garnish:
Crisp lettuce and sliced tomatoes

1 First prepare the hamburgers. In a bowl combine the beef, onion, stock cube, salt and pepper to taste and the herbs. Bind together well with the egg, then divide into four equal portions and shape into hamburgers.

2 Heat a grill or a barbecue and grill the hamburgers for about 5 minutes on each side, depending on how you like your hamburgers cooked. Remove and keep warm.

3 Heat the oil in a non-stick frying pan and fry the mushrooms for about 1 minute. Add the horseradish and salt and pepper and heat through. Spoon on top of the hamburgers and sprinkle with the cheese. Place under the grill until the cheese melts.

Serving suggestion: Line a large serving dish or individual dishes with lettuce leaves and arrange the hamburgers on top. Garnish with slices of tomato and serve immediately.

Stuffed Tomatoes

Serves 6
Preparation time: 15 minutes
Calories per serving: 65 (272 kilojoules)

At 65 calories you can afford to have more than one of these.

3 ripe, firm tomatoes
350g/12oz cottage cheese
100g/4oz carrot, grated
100g/4oz cucumber, peeled and grated
75g/3oz finely-chopped spring onion
4 radishes, grated

Salt and freshly-ground black pepper
1 tablespoon low-calorie salad dressing

To serve:
Crisp lettuce and fresh parsley

1 Cut each tomato in half horizontally and, with a spoon, scoop out and reserve the pulp and seeds.

2 In a bowl, combine together the cottage cheese, cucumber, spring onion, radishes and salt and pepper. Add the salad dressing and mix together well.

3 Spoon equal amounts of the filling into the tomato halves. Arrange the lettuce leaves on a serving dish or individual plates and place the stuffed tomatoes on top.

Serving suggestion: Serve garnished with fresh parsley.

Swiss Sole Soufflé

Serve this light-as-a-feather soufflé with your favourite sauce. I suggest something with a little touch of spice.

Serves 2
Preparation time: 30 minutes
Cooking time: 20–25 minutes
Calories per serving: 220 (921 kilojoules)

100g/4oz fillet of sole
8 tablespoons water
1 tablespoon cornflour
1 teaspoon Dijon mustard
2 teaspoons lemon juice
Salt and freshly-ground black pepper

50g/1oz Gruyère or Emmental cheese, grated
2 egg yolks, beaten
2 tablespoons freshly-chopped parsley
3 egg whites

Pre-heat the oven to 190°C/375°F/Gas Mark 5

1   Lightly butter two individual soufflé dishes.

2   Place the sole in a blender or food processor and purée with 4 tablespoons water. In a small bowl dissolve the cornflour in 1 tablespoon water. Heat the remaining 3 tablespoons water in a small saucepan with the mustard, lemon juice, salt and pepper. Stir in the dissolved cornflour and whisk over the heat until thick. Add to the fish purée, blend together well then transfer the mixture back to the saucepan. Stir over a medium heat for 1 minute.

3   Remove the pan from the heat and mix in 2 tablespoons of the cheese, the egg yolks and the parsley.

4   Using an electric mixer, beat the egg whites until stiff then fold carefully into the fish mixture. Spoon the mixture into the prepared soufflé dishes and sprinkle the tops with the remaining cheese. Bake for about 20–25 minutes or until puffed and golden.

Serving suggestion: Serve the soufflés immediately with your favourite spicy sauce.

Strawberry Cheesecake

Serves 12
Preparation time: 40 minutes (plus chilling time)
Calories per serving: 195 (1236 kilojoules)

When you're on a diet and dreaming of cheesecake, here's a recipe you don't have to feel guilty about.

6 digestive biscuits, crushed
6 Melba toasts, crushed
7 individual packets low-calorie sweetener
¾ teaspoon cinnamon
2 tablespoons margarine, melted
1 large can crushed pineapple in natural juice
2 envelopes unflavoured gelatine

2 eggs, separated
225ml/8fl oz plain yoghurt
675g/1½lb Ricotta cheese
2 tablespoons lemon juice
1½ teaspoons finely-grated lemon rind
65g/2½oz sugar
1 teaspoon cornflour

To garnish:
150g/5oz fresh strawberries

Pre-heat the oven to 190°C/375°F/Gas Mark 5

1   In a bowl combine together the crushed digestive biscuits, Melba toasts, 1 packet low-calorie sweetener and the cinnamon. Stir in the melted margarine. Press into the bottom of a 20cm/8in springform tin and bake for 6 minutes. Allow to cool.

2   In a saucepan combine 50ml/2fl oz of the juice from the pineapple with the gelatine and the remaining sweetener. Allow to stand for a few minutes then place over a low heat until the gelatine dissolves. Remove from the heat.

3   In a bowl, beat the egg yolks and gradually beat in the gelatine mixture. In a blender or food processor blend together the yoghurt and half the Ricotta cheese until smooth. Transfer to a large bowl. In the blender or food processor blend together the remaining Ricotta, the egg yolk mixture, lemon juice and lemon rind. Add this to the yoghurt mixture.

4   In a bowl whisk the egg whites until stiff, gradually adding the sugar. Fold into the cheese mixture and pour into the cooled crust. Cover and chill for at least 4 hours.

5   Combine the cornflour with the remaining pineapple and juice in a saucepan. Stir over a medium heat until thickened. Place the saucepan in a bowl of cold water and allow to cool. Spoon over the cheesecake and chill for 30 minutes before serving.

Serving suggestion: Serve the cheesecake garnished with fresh strawberries.

Chicken and Parmesan Stir Fry

If you have all the ingredients prepared beforehand, you can cook this simple dish right in front of your guests.

Serves 4
Preparation time: 30 minutes
Cooking time: About 10 minutes
Calories per serving: 175 (730 kilojoules)

450g/1lb chicken breasts, skinned, boned and trimmed
900g/2lb broccoli florets
2 tablespoons olive oil
1 large onion, sliced
2 red peppers, cut into strips
2 large garlic cloves, crushed

1 teaspoon dried basil, crumbled
½ teaspoon dried thyme, crumbled
¼ teaspoon dried rosemary, crumbled
Salt and freshly-ground black pepper
4 tablespoons freshly-grated Parmesan cheese

1   First place the chicken between sheets of greaseproof paper and, using a rolling pin, pound to a thickness of 5mm/¼in. Cover and freeze until just firm, then cut into strips. Place the broccoli in a bowl and cover with cold water.

2 Heat the oil in a wok or large frying pan, then add the onion, red pepper, garlic, herbs and freshly-ground black pepper. Stir fry for 2 minutes then add the broccoli straight from the water. Stir fry for a further 3 minutes. Reduce the heat, cover and allow to steam for 2 minutes.

3 Add the chicken and a little salt. Cover and continue to steam until the chicken is cooked, about 1 minute. Uncover the pan, increase the heat and stir fry until the liquid reduces slightly, about a further minute. Sprinkle over the Parmesan cheese and serve immediately.

Serving suggestion: Serve this dish with plenty of boiled rice.

Vegetable-Stuffed Crêpes

**Serves 4
Preparation time: 40 minutes
Calories per serving: 300 (1256 kilojoules)**

Be a bit adventurous – fill these light pancakes with any of your favourite vegetables.

For the filling:
1 onion, finely chopped
6 tomatoes, skinned and chopped
100g/4oz thin green beans, trimmed
100g/4oz mushrooms, sliced
1 teaspoon mixed herbs
Salt and freshly-ground black pepper

For the pancakes:
100g/4oz plain flour

Pinch of salt
275ml/½ pint skimmed milk
1 egg
1 tablespoon vegetable oil

For the topping:
100g/4oz Lancashire cheese, grated

To garnish:
Freshly-chopped parsley

1 First make the filling. Place all the ingredients in a saucepan, bring to the boil then cover and simmer for about 10 minutes.

2 Meanwhile make the pancakes. Sift the flour with the salt into a bowl. Make a well in the middle, add half the milk and the egg then beat together until smooth. Add the remaining milk and stir in.

3 Lightly grease an 18cm/7in frying pan. Heat over a medium heat and pour in just enough pancake batter to coat the base. Cook until just lightly browned, then toss or turn and cook the other side. Repeat with the remaining batter to make 8 pancakes, stacking them between greaseproof paper to keep them warm and separate.

4 Divide the filling between the pancakes and sprinkle with a little of the cheese. Fold them up and sprinkle the top with the remaining cheese. Arrange on a heatproof dish and place under a hot grill until the cheese melts and is bubbly.

Serving suggestion: Serve immediately garnished with fresh parsley.

Baked Stuffed Parmesan Mushrooms

These stuffed mushrooms make a great low–calorie starter.

12 large white mushrooms
1 teaspoon vegetable oil
1 small onion, very finely chopped
Salt and freshly-ground black pepper
2 tablespoons freshly-grated Parmesan cheese
1 tablespoon finely-chopped fresh parsley

Serves 6
Preparation time: 15 minutes
Cooking time: 12 minutes
Calories per mushroom: 37 (151 kilojoules)

1 Wipe the mushrooms clean and cut off the stem end. Carefully remove the stems and chop very finely.

2   Heat the oil in a frying pan and sauté the chopped mushroom stems with the onion for about 10 minutes over a low heat. Add salt and pepper to taste, the Parmesan cheese and the parsley. Stir well and remove from the heat.

Pre-heat the oven to 190°C/375°F/Gas Mark 5

3   Stuff each mushroom cap with this mixture, arrange on a lightly-oiled baking tray and bake for 12 minutes.

Serving suggestion: Serve the mushrooms immediately.

Baked Potatoes
Stuffed with Cottage Cheese

Serves 4
Preparation time: 15 minutes
Cooking time: 1 hour
Calories per serving: 120 (520 kilojoules)

There's a mere 17 calories (72 kilojoules) per tablespoon in this cottage cheese topping.

4 medium baking potatoes
A little vegetable oil
Salt

For the topping:
100g/4oz cottage cheese

50ml/2fl oz soured cream
1 tablespoon freshly-chopped chives
Salt and freshly-ground black pepper

Pre-heat the oven to 220°C/425°F/Gas Mark 7

1   Scrub the potatoes under cold water and pat dry. Prick all over with a fork and cover very lightly in vegetable oil. Place on a baking tray and bake for about 1 hour or until the potatoes feel soft when squeezed.

2   Meanwhile, make the topping. Place all the ingredients in a blender or food processor and blend until smooth.

3   When ready to serve, slash an X with a sharp knife in the top of each potato and squeeze (using a clean tea towel as they will be very hot) so that the potatoes fluff up.

Serving suggestion: Serve the hot potatoes immediately with a large spoonful of the topping.

Cheesey Coleslaw

If you have a food processor, this side dish can be made even more quickly! Here's an excellent idea for a summer barbecue.

Serves 4
Preparation time: 20 minutes
Calories per serving: 220 (921 kilojoules)

2 carrots, peeled
2 sticks tender celery
225g/8oz white cabbage
1 sweet apple, peeled and cored
50g/2oz raisins
2 teaspoons lemon juice
175g/6oz Gouda or mature Cheddar cheese, grated

150g/5oz plain, low-fat yoghurt
Salt and freshly-ground black pepper

To garnish:
Fresh parsley

1   Grate the carrots, using a food processor, or by hand, and place in a bowl. Grate the celery and cabbage and mix in with the carrot. Grate the apple and add to the rest with the raisins. Sprinkle with the lemon juice and toss together well.

2   In a small bowl mix together the cheese, yoghurt and salt and pepper until smooth. Stir into the salad until completely covered. Transfer to a large serving bowl and serve.

Serving suggestion: Serve garnished with fresh parsley.

Grilled Open-Faced Sandwiches

Serves 4
Preparation time: 20 minutes
Calories per serving: 275 (1151 kilojoules)

A perfect light luncheon dish.

4 slices wholewheat bread
Low-calorie margarine
2 apples, peeled and cored
4 thin slices ham
2 tablespoons sweet pickle
4 spring onions, finely chopped

100g/4oz Lancashire or mature Cheddar cheese, grated

To garnish:
Fresh parsley sprigs

1   First lightly toast the bread on both sides and spread with a little low-calorie margarine.

2   Slice the apples thinly and arrange on the bread. Top each with a slice of ham and spread with a little pickle. Sprinkle evenly with the chopped spring onions.

3   Sprinkle each sandwich with some cheese. Place under a pre-heated grill and leave until heated through – the cheese should be bubbling and golden-brown. Serve immediately.

Serving suggestion: Serve each sandwich with a sprig of fresh parsley.

Stuffed Pasta Shells

These pasta shells are stuffed with a low-calorie tomato, red pepper and chilli sauce and topped with Parmesan or Romano cheese.

Serves 2–4
Preparation time: 30 minutes
Calories per serving: 335 (1424 kilojoules)

1 red pepper
½ chilli pepper, seeds removed
1 medium onion, chopped
1 large can plum tomatoes, drained
1 teaspoon sugar
Salt and freshly-ground black pepper

175g/6oz freshly-cooked pasta shells
25g/1oz freshly-chopped parsley
100g/4oz freshly-grated Parmesan or Romano cheese

1 Place the red pepper under a hot grill and char on all sides until blackened. Place in a paper bag and leave for 10 minutes to steam. Peel and remove all the seeds and pith, then cut into pieces.

2 Using a blender or food processor, thoroughly mince the chilli pepper. Add the onion, drained tomatoes and the red pepper and chop coarsely. Transfer the mixture to a large saucepan.

3 Add the sugar, salt and pepper and stir over a medium heat until the onion softens, stirring for about 10 minutes. Adjust the seasoning to taste.

4 Place the freshly-cooked pasta in a large bowl, pour over the sauce and toss completely. Spoon on to individual plates, sprinkle with fresh parsley and the grated cheese.

Serving suggestion: Serve immediately.

Cheddar Baked Cod

Serves 4
Preparation time: 20 minutes
Cooking time: 30 minutes
Calories per serving: 245 (1026 kilojoules)

Serve this dish with boiled rice and you will have a very wholesome meal for all the family.

4 cod cutlets
A little fresh lemon juice
Salt and freshly-ground black pepper

75g/3oz mature Cheddar cheese, grated
Pinch of paprika

For the cheese sauce:
25g/1oz plain flour
275ml/½ pint skimmed milk

To garnish
1 tomato, quartered
parsley sprigs

1 First prepare the cod. Rinse under cold water and pat dry with paper towels. Place in an ovenproof dish, sprinkle with a little lemon juice and season with salt and pepper.

2 To make the sauce, melt the margarine in a saucepan and stir in the flour. Stir together over a medium heat for 1 minute, then remove from the heat and slowly add the milk, stirring continuously. Return to the heat and stir until the sauce thickens. Stir in the cheese and paprika, and a little salt and pepper to taste, and stir until the cheese melts.

Pre-heat the oven to 180°C/350°F/Gas Mark 4

3 Pour the sauce over the cod and bake for 30 minutes.

Serving suggestion: Serve this dish garnished with tomato quarters and fresh parsley sprigs.

Cauliflower Cheese

I just love this combination – slightly crisp cauliflower with hot and bubbly cheese. For me this can be a meal in itself, but it also makes an ideal accompaniment.

Serves 4
Preparation time: 25 minutes
Cooking time: 30 minutes
Calories per serving: 135 (565 kilojoules)

1 cauliflower
Salt and freshly-ground black pepper
150ml/¼ pint skimmed milk

75g/3oz mature Cheddar cheese, grated
1 egg, beaten
1 teaspoon paprika
1 tomato, sliced

1   Trim all the leaves from the cauliflower and cut off the stem. Wash under cold water and drain. Break the cauliflower into florets, place in a saucepan of boiling salted water and cook for 5 minutes. Drain.

2   In a bowl beat together the milk, half the cheese, the egg and salt and pepper to taste.

Pre-heat the oven to 180°C/350°F/Gas Mark 4

3   Place the cauliflower florets in an ovenproof dish and pour the egg mixture over the top. Sprinkle with the remaining cheese and bake for about 30 minutes or until the cheese sauce has set. Garnish with sliced tomato and serve immediately.

Note: To make this dish a little more substantial, you can add 225g/8oz chopped ham to the cheese sauce.

7
Desserts

What better way to end a meal than with a creamy slice of cheesecake, or a big slice of hot apple pie lined with cheese pastry? How about a wonderful pound cake at teatime, or carrot cake with cream cheese frosting? There really are wonderful desserts that can be made using cheeses, and I have crammed this chapter full with my favourites to share with you. I have included several different types of cheesecakes and flans (including one using Cheddar!) which may not necessarily be too good for slimmers, but all such a temptation. Try the little Date and Cream Cheese Pastries, ideal to take on a picnic, and the very easy but attractive Cherry Cream Cheese Crown for a real hit with family and friends. No matter what the occasion, I'm sure you'll find something ideal to highlight it right here.

Carrot Cake with Cream Cheese Frosting

This is the moistest carrot cake you'll ever taste.

Serves 8–10
Preparation time: 25 minutes
Cooking time: 30–40 minutes

275ml/½ pint vegetable oil
225g/8oz brown sugar
200g/7oz caster sugar
4 eggs
150g/5oz plain flour
100g/4oz less 2 tablespoons wholewheat flour
1 teaspoon salt
2 teaspoons baking soda
2 teaspoons baking powder
2 teaspoons cinnamon
350g/12oz grated carrot
225g/8oz can crushed pineapple in natural juice, drained
50g/2oz chopped walnuts

For the cream cheese frosting:
225g/8oz cream cheese, softened
50g/2oz unsalted butter, softened
225g/8oz confectioner's sugar
1½ teaspoons vanilla
1 tablespoon finely-grated lemon rind

1   In a large bowl blend together the oil and both sugars. Add one egg at a time and blend together well.

2   Sift together the flours, salt, baking soda, baking powder and cinnamon in another bowl. Add a little of the oil mixture at a time, beating just to blend. Fold in the grated carrot, the pineapple and the nuts.

Pre-heat the oven to 180°C/350°F/Gas Mark 4

3   Lightly grease a 30cm/12in square tin (*see* note). Line the tin with greaseproof paper and spoon in the cake mixture. Level the top, place in the oven and bake for 30–40 minutes or until a cake tester inserted in the centre comes out clean. Allow to cool in the tin before transferring to a cooling rack.

4   To make the frosting, mash the cream cheese until smooth, then add the butter and cream together until fluffy. Add the vanilla and the lemon rind and cream together.

5   When the cake is cool, spread the frosting over the top and cut into squares. Serve immediately or keep covered in the refrigerator.

Note: Try using two 20cm/8in round cake tins and make a layer cake sandwiched with the frosting.

Cheese-Filled Blintzes

**Makes 10
Preparation
time: 30
minutes (plus
refrigeration
time)**

Blintzes are a Jewish speciality and can be prepared with a variety of fillings but, for me, cheese-filled blintzes are the best.

For the filling:
*75g/3oz packet cottage
   cheese, softened*
*450g/1lb cottage or Ricotta
   cheese*
1 egg yolk
2 tablespoons sugar
½ teaspoon vanilla essence

For the blintzes:
2 eggs
2 tablespoons vegetable oil
225ml/8fl oz milk
75g/3oz sifted plain flour
½ teaspoon salt
50g/2oz butter

To serve:
*Icing sugar and soured
   cream*

1   First make the filling. In a bowl, combine together the cheeses, egg yolk, sugar and vanilla. Beat together thoroughly with an electric mixer until completely smooth. Cover and refrigerate while making the blintzes.

2   In a bowl beat together the eggs, oil and milk until well mixed. Add the flour and salt and beat together until smooth. Cover and refrigerate for 30 minutes.

3   Make one blintze at a time. Melt ½ teaspoon butter in a 25cm/10in frying pan and pour in 3 tablespoons batter to cover the entire base of the pan. Cook over a moderate heat until lightly browned on underside, then remove and stack, browned side up.

4   Place about 3 tablespoons of the cheese filling on the browned side of each blintze, fold opposite sides over the filling and overlap the ends. Make sure the filling is covered completely.

5   Melt the remaining butter in a large frying pan and add 3 or 4 blintzes at a time. Sauté until golden-brown on the underside, then turn and sauté the other side. Keep warm in the oven while cooking the remaining blintzes.

Serving suggestion: Serve the blintzes warm, dusted with icing sugar and each with a dollop of soured cream.

Creamy Pound Cake

The traditional American 'pound cake' was exactly that – a cake recipe in which all the ingredients used (flour, sugar, butter and eggs) were 450g/1lb in weight. Here is a variation on that tradition that also includes cream cheese.

Serves 10–12
Preparation time: 20 minutes
Cooking time: 1 hour 15 minutes

225g/8oz packet cream cheese, softened
225g/8oz margarine, softened
100g/4oz unsalted butter, softened

600g/1lb 5oz sugar
6 eggs
350g/12oz less 3 tablespoons plain flour
2 teaspoons vanilla essence

Pre-heat the oven to 180°C/350°F/Gas Mark 4

1   Lightly grease and flour a 2.5 litre/4 pint fluted ring cake tin.

2   In a large bowl beat the cream cheese with the margarine, butter and sugar until very smooth. Add the eggs, one at a time, alternating with the flour, and stir well between each addition. Stir in the vanilla.

3   Pour the batter into the prepared tin and bake for 30 minutes. Reduce the oven temperature to 170°C/325°F/Gas Mark 3 and continue to bake for about 45 minutes, or until a cake tester inserted in the centre comes out clean.

4   Allow the cake to cool in the tin on a cooling rack, then invert on to a serving dish.

Serving suggestion: Serve this cake at room temperature.

Custard Cheese Flan

Serves 8
Preparation time: 35 minutes
Cooking time: 1 hour 20 minutes

This custard flan is baked with a caramel on the bottom, then you invert it on to a serving dish and *voilà!*

For the caramel:
200g/7oz sugar
125ml/4fl oz water

For the custard:
400ml/14fl oz water

400g/14oz can sweetened condensed milk
6 eggs
225g/8oz packet cream cheese, softened

Pre-heat the oven to 150°C/300°F/Gas Mark 2

1   Place the sugar and water in a saucepan over a low heat until the sugar dissolves, swirling the pan occasionally. Bring to the boil and boil until the syrup turns golden-brown, about 8 minutes. Pour into a 23cm/9in glass baking dish and tilt the dish so the caramel coats the bottom. Allow to cool completely.

2   Using a blender or food processor, blend to-
    gether all the custard ingredients until smooth.
    Pour into the caramel dish.

3   Place the dish in a large baking pan and add
    enough hot water to come three-quarters of the
    way up the side of the dish. Bake for about 1
    hour 20 minutes, or until a cake tester inserted
    in the centre comes out clean. Cool, then cover
    and chill thoroughly.

4   When ready to serve, gently loosen the sides of
    the custard with the back of a spoon then invert
    on to a serving dish.

Serving suggestion: Serve chilled.

Cottage Cheese Dumplings

This light and not-too-sweet dessert is best served
with a fresh fruit compôte. Choose your favourite
fruit, depending on the time of year.

Serves 10
**Preparation
time: 20
minutes (plus
standing time)
Cooking time:
10 minutes**

*675g/1½lb cottage cheese,
    drained*
3 eggs
50g/2oz butter, melted
*150g/5oz fresh white
    breadcrumbs*
*2 tablespoons fresh lemon
    juice*
3 tablespoons sugar

*½ teaspoon finely-grated
    lemon rind*
Pinch of salt

For the coating:
*Lightly-toasted
    breadcrumbs, mixed
    with sugar*

1   In a large bowl mix together the cottage cheese,
    eggs and butter until thoroughly combined.
    Leave aside for 20 minutes.

2   Add to the mixture the fresh breadcrumbs,
    lemon juice, sugar, lemon rind and salt and
    blend together well. Allow the batter to stand
    for 20 minutes.

3 Bring a large saucepan of salted water to the boil. Form the batter into 3cm/1½in balls. Using a slotted spoon, lower the dumplings into the boiling water and poach for about 10 minutes until firm. Don't put all the dumplings in at once. Remove using the slotted spoon and immediately coat with the sweetened breadcrumbs.

Serving suggestion: Serve immediately with your favourite fruit compôte.

Quick Chocolate Chip Cheesecake

Serves 10–12
Preparation time: 15 minutes
Cooking time: 45 minutes

Believe it or not, here is a delicious cheesecake that can be made in just 15 minutes. A perfect last-minute dessert.

For the biscuit crust:
150g/5oz 'Digestive' biscuits, crushed
75g/3oz unsalted butter, melted

For the cheesecake:
3 × 225g/8oz packets cream cheese, softened
75g/3oz sugar
3 eggs
175g/6oz plain chocolate chips
1 teaspoon vanilla essence

1 First make the biscuit crust. Combine the crushed biscuits and the melted butter in a bowl. Press into the bottom of a 23cm/9in springform tin. Chill in the refrigerator.

2 Meanwhile, in a large bowl combine the cream cheese and the sugar. Using an electric mixer, mix until well blended. Add the eggs, one at a time, mixing well between each addition. Stir in the chocolate chips and the vanilla.

Pre-heat the oven to 230°C/450°F/Gas Mark 8

3 Pour the mixture over the prepared crust and bake for 10 minutes. Reduce the oven temperature to 130°C/250°F/Gas Mark 4 and continue to bake for 35 minutes. Remove the cake from the oven and loosen the sides of the tin. Allow to cool before removing the cake.

Serving suggestion: This cheesecake is best served chilled.

No-Fail Cheesecake

It isn't the fact that this cheesecake never fails that makes it so special – it's absolutely delicious and the soured cream topping is a knockout!

Serves 10–12
Preparation time: 25 minutes
Cooking time: 30 minutes

For the crust:
225g/8oz 'Hob-nob' biscuits, crushed
100g/4oz butter or margarine, melted

For the cheesecake
3 × 225g/8oz packets cream cheese, softened

5 eggs
200g/7oz sugar
1 teaspoon lemon juice
1 teaspoon vanilla essence

For the topping:
1 litre/1 ¾ pints soured cream
200g/7oz sugar
1 teaspoon vanilla essence

1 First make the crust. Combine the crushed biscuits with the melted butter and press into the bottom of a 25cm/10in springform tin. Chill.

Pre-heat the oven to 180°C/350°F/Gas Mark 4

2 Place together in a large bowl the cream cheese, eggs, sugar, lemon juice and vanilla and beat together using an electric mixer until smooth. Pour into the prepared crust and bake for 20 minutes. Turn the oven off and leave the cheesecake to stand in the oven for 1 hour.

3   Remove from the oven and increase the oven temperature to 240°C/475°F/Gas Mark 9.

4   In a bowl mix together the soured cream, sugar and vanilla. Spread over the top of the cake and bake for about 10 minutes until the edges begin to bubble. Cool in the pan before removing.

Serving suggestion: Serve this cheesecake thoroughly chilled.

American Apple Pie with Cheese Pastry

Serves 8
Preparation time: 35 minutes (plus chilling time)
Cooking time: 45 minutes

Americans invented the wonderful combination of hot, juicy apple pie topped with a slice of melted cheese. Here's a fun alternative – a deep-dish fruit pie covered in a cheese pastry.

For the cheese pastry:
350g/12oz plain flour
Pinch of salt
100g/4oz butter, chilled
50g/2oz Cheddar cheese, grated
Cold water, to bind

For the apple filling:
1125g/2½lb cooking apples, peeled, cored and sliced

150g/5oz sugar
3 tablespoons flour
½ teaspoon cinnamon
¼ teaspoon freshly-grated nutmeg
½ teaspoon finely-grated lemon rind
1 tablespoon butter or margarine
Milk, to glaze

1   First make the pastry. In a bowl sift together the flour and salt. Add the butter and rub in until the mixture resembles fine breadcrumbs. Add the cheese and mix in thoroughly. Add cold water a little at a time and mix in using a knife until a firm dough is formed. Cover and chill for 30 minutes.

2 Roll out the pastry to fit the base of a 23cm/9in pie dish and to form a lid.

Pre-heat the oven to 220°C/425°F/Gas Mark 7

3 Place the apple slices in a large bowl. In a small bowl combine together the sugar, flour, cinnamon, nutmeg and lemon rind. Sprinkle over the apple and toss together until all the apple is coated. Transfer to the pie dish and dot with the butter.

4 Use the remaining pastry to fit as a lid. Seal the edges and cut a few slits in the top to allow steam to escape. Use any leftover pastry to decorate the top. Brush the top with the milk.

5 Bake the pie for about 45 minutes or until the pastry is golden-brown.

Serving suggestion: Serve the pie hot, warm or cold.

Date and Cream Cheese Pastries

Makes 25
Preparation
time: 1 hour
(plus overnight
chilling)
Cooking time:
20 minutes

These little pastries are a perfect teatime treat.

For the pastry:
225g/8oz unsalted butter,
    softened
225g/8oz cream cheese,
    softened
225g/8oz plain flour

For the date paste:
225g/8oz dried dates,
    pitted and chopped
225ml/8fl oz water
100g/4oz unsalted butter,
    cut into pieces
1 teaspoon vanilla essence
1 teaspoon cinnamon
2 tablespoons lemon juice

1 First make the pastry the day before assembling. Cream together the butter and cream cheese using an electric hand mixer. Add the flour and mix together to form a dough. Knead on a lightly-floured surface, cover with greaseproof paper and chill overnight.

2 To make the date paste, simmer the dates and water for about 12 minutes until the water evaporates. Continue to stir over the heat, until the mixture forms a paste. Add the butter and stir for about 5 minutes until the mixture pulls away from the sides of the pan. Add the vanilla, cinnamon and lemon juice. Spread the paste out on a platter, cool and then chill until very firm.

3 Allow the pastry to stand at room temperature for 30 minutes.

Pre-heat the oven to 200°C/400°F/Gas Mark 6

4 Roll out the pastry to about 2mm/⅛in thickness and cut out 5cm/2in rounds using a biscuit cutter. Assemble on a baking tray and chill briefly.

5 Place a teaspoon of date paste in the centre of half of the rounds and top each with another round. Press the edges to seal and brush lightly with the glaze. Bake for about 20 minutes until golden-brown. Allow to cool slightly and serve warm.

Note: These pastries can be assembled right up to baking, about 1 week ahead. Cover and freeze but don't thaw before cooking.

Frozen Ricotta Dessert

Ideally, this dessert is made using an ice cream machine, but I have given instructions to use if you don't own one. Start preparing this dessert two days before you plan to serve it.

**Serves 8
Preparation
time: 30
minutes (plus
two days'
refrigeration)**

*850g/1lb 14oz Ricotta
   cheese
100g/4oz icing sugar
125ml/4fl oz water
175ml/6fl oz whipping
   cream, well chilled
1 tablespoon vanilla
   essence*

2 tablespoons rum

To serve:
*Candied fruit
Chopped nuts
Fresh pears and figs*

1 Beat the Ricotta cheese using an electric mixer until very smooth and fluffy. Beat the sugar in slowly, then cover and refrigerate for 2 days.

2 Whisk the water into the chilled cheese. In another bowl, whip the cream until soft peaks form. Fold in the vanilla and rum, then fold the cream mixture into the cheese. Cover and refrigerate until well chilled.

3 If you are using an ice cream machine, process this mixture according to the manufacturer's instructions. Transfer to a covered container and freeze for several hours.

4 If making by hand, spoon the mixture into an airtight container and freeze for 3–4 hours, stirring twice to prevent crystals forming. Allow the dessert to soften slightly in the refrigerator before serving.

Serving suggestion: Serve scoops of this with candied fruit, chopped nuts or fresh pears and figs.

Baked
Cottage Cheese Surprise

Serves 6
Preparation time: 25 minutes
Cooking time: 40 minutes

This cottage cheese custard is made extra special by the variety of accompaniments. Serve it so that your guests can help themselves to toppings.

1 tablespoon unsalted butter, softened
4 eggs
450ml/16fl oz single cream
25g/1oz plain flour
6 tablespoons sugar
1 teaspoon vanilla essence
Pinch of salt
Pinch of freshly-grated nutmeg

450g/1lb cottage cheese
1 tablespoon sugar

Accompaniments:
Fresh berries
Soured cream
Plain yoghurt
Brown sugar
Cinnamon sugar

Pre-heat the oven to 220°C/425°F/Gas Mark 7

1 Spread the butter over the sides and bottom of a 2.5 litre/4 pint soufflé dish. Dust all over with 1 tablespoon sugar.

2 Combine all but the final 2 ingredients in a blender or food processor until completely smooth. Add the cottage cheese and blend slowly to just combine. Pour the mixture into the prepared dish and bake for 30 minutes.

3   Reduce the oven temperature to 180°C/350°F/ Gas Mark 4 and bake for a further 10 minutes. Sprinkle the top with the 1 tablespoon sugar and bake until a cake tester inserted in the centre comes out clean, about 5 minutes. Allow to cool for 10 minutes before serving.

Serving suggestion: Serve the accompaniments in separate bowls with the custard and allow your guests to help themselves.

Lemon Cheese Pie

Here's a sweet cheese pie with a fresh hint of lemon.

For the crust:
175g/6oz 'Digestive'
  biscuits, crushed
75g/3oz butter, melted

For the pie:
3 eggs
75g/3oz sugar
225g/8oz packet cream
  cheese, softened

100g/4oz cottage cheese

For the topping:
400g/14oz can sweetened
  condensed milk
50ml/2fl oz fresh lemon
  juice

To garnish:
Grated lemon rind

**Serves 6–8
Preparation time: 30 minutes (plus chilling overnight)
Cooking time: 35 minutes**

1   First make the crust. Combine the crushed biscuits with the melted butter and press into the bottom of a 23cm/9in pie dish. Chill.

Pre-heat the oven to 180°C/350°F/Gas Mark 4

2   Beat the eggs using an electric mixer until thick, about 3 minutes. Add the sugar slowly and beat in. Add the cream and cottage cheese and blend together until smooth.

3   Pour the mixture into the prepared pie crust and bake for 35 minutes. Allow the pie to cool for 15 minutes.

4 To make the topping, combine the condensed milk with the lemon juice. Spread over the top of the pie, cover and refrigerate overnight.

Serving suggestion: To serve, garnish the top of the pie with grated lemon rind. Serve chilled.

Pineapple Cheese Tart

**Serves 6–8
Preparation
time: 30
minutes (plus
overnight
refrigeration)**

This no-cook cheese tart combines the delicious flavours of pineapple, chocolate and orange – magic!

For the crust:
*175g/6oz plain chocolate
'Hob-nob' biscuits,
crushed
75g/3oz unsalted butter or
margarine, melted*

For the tart:
*575ml/20fl oz can crushed
pineapple in syrup
225g/8oz packet cream
cheese, softened*

*2 tablespoons fresh orange
juice
4 teaspoons finely-grated
orange rind
3 tablespoons orange
liqueur
3 tablespoons sugar
1 tablespoon cornflour
Thin slices of orange and
fresh mint leaves*

1 To make the crust, combine the crushed biscuits with the melted butter and press into the bottom of a 23cm/9in springform tin. Chill.

2 Meanwhile, to make the tart first drain 2 tablespoons of the syrup from the tinned pineapple, and pour the remaining undrained pineapple into a saucepan.

3 Using an electric mixer, beat together in a bowl the cream cheese, the 2 tablespoons reserved pineapple syrup, the orange juice, 1 tablespoon of the orange rind, 2 tablespoons of the liqueur and the sugar until smooth. Pour into the prepared crust and refrigerate overnight.

4 Add the cornflour and the remaining 1 teaspoon orange rind and 1 tablespoon orange liqueur to the pineapple in the saucepan, and cook over a moderate heat, stirring, until thickened and clear. Allow to cool.

5 Spoon this sauce over the top of the tart and serve.

Serving suggestion: Serve the tart garnished with thin slices of orange and fresh mint leaves.

Mature Cheddar Cheesecake

At last, a sweet cheesecake with a difference.

For the crust:
175g/6oz 'Digestive' biscuits, crushed
75g/3oz butter, melted

For the cheesecake:
275g/10oz sugar

4 × 225g/8oz cream cheese, softened
6 eggs
50ml/2fl oz soured cream
175g/6oz mature Cheddar cheese, grated
50ml/2fl oz beer
3 tablespoons cornflour

Serves 10
Preparation time: 25 minutes
Cooking time: 1 hour

1 First make the biscuit crust. Combine together the crushed biscuits and the melted butter. Press into the bottom of a 23cm/9in springform tin. Set aside.

Pre-heat the oven to 170°C/325°F/Gas Mark 5

2 In a blender or food processor, combine the sugar, cream cheese, eggs, soured cream, Cheddar, beer and cornflour until smooth. Pour into the prepared crust and bake for 1 hour, or until a cake tester inserted in the centre comes out clean. Turn the oven off and allow the cake to cool completely while still in the oven with the door slightly open.

3   Cover the cake and chill thoroughly before serving.

Serving suggestion: This cheesecake should be served chilled.

Individual Cheesecakes

Makes 2
Preparation time: 15 minutes
Cooking time: 35–40 minutes

These little cheesecakes are made in individual ramekins – they're perfect for a dinner for two.

2 × 75g/3oz packets cream cheese, softened
75g/3oz sugar
2 eggs
1 teaspoon lemon juice

1 teaspoon vanilla essence

To serve:
Soured cream
Grated plain chocolate

Pre-heat the oven to 180°C/350°F/Gas Mark 4

1   Lightly butter two 225ml/8fl oz ramekins.

2   Using a blender or food processor, blend together the cream cheese, sugar, eggs, vanilla and lemon juice until smooth. Divide the mixture between the two prepared ramekins and bake until the tops are golden-brown and a cake tester inserted in the centre comes out clean – about 35–40 minutes.

3   Allow the cheesecakes to cool, then chill completely before serving.

Serving suggestion: Remove the cheesecakes from the ramekins on to individual serving dishes. Dollop some soured cream on top and sprinkle with grated chocolate. Serve immediately.

Note: These cheesecakes can be made 2 hours in advance if kept covered in the refrigerator.

Brie Tart

This recipe I found is based on a medieval recipe that was most probably used in Norman times.

Serves 6–8
Preparation time: 40 minutes
Cooking time: About 40 minutes

For the pastry:
175g/6oz plain flour
Pinch of salt
75g/3oz half lard, half unsalted butter
Cold water, to combine

For the tart:
225g/8oz fresh, runny Brie
4 egg yolks
¼ teaspoon cinnamon
¼ teaspoon ground ginger
1 tablespoon runny honey
Pinch of saffron

1   First make the pastry. Sift the flour and salt into a bowl. Cut the fat into pieces and add to the flour. Rub in until the mixture resembles fine breadcrumbs. Add spoonfuls of cold water and stir with a knife until a firm dough forms. Cover in clingfilm and chill for 20 minutes.

Pre-heat the oven to 180°C/350°F/Gas Mark 4

2   Roll out the chilled dough on a lightly-floured surface and line a 20cm/8in pie plate. Bake blind for 15 minutes, then remove the paper and beans and bake a further 5–10 minutes.

3   Meanwhile, make the tart. Remove the rind from the cheese and discard. Place the cheese in a bowl and mix together with the egg yolks until thoroughly combined. Add all the remaining ingredients and combine well.

4   Pour the mixture into the pastry case and bake for 20–30 minutes, or until a cake tester inserted in the centre comes out clean.

Serving suggestion: Serve this tart immediately.

Exceptionally-Rich Mocha Cheesecake

Serves 10–12
Preparation time: 30 minutes
Cooking time: 2 hours

This may be the richest cheesecake you ever eat, but I promise you it's worth its weight in gold!

For the chocolate biscuit crust:
175g/6oz plain chocolate 'Digestive' biscuits, crushed
75g/3oz unsalted butter, melted

For the cheesecake:
675g/1½lb cream cheese, softened

200g/7oz sugar
4 eggs
70ml/2½fl oz whipping cream
1 teaspoon vanilla essence
1 tablespoon instant coffee powder
175g/6oz plain chocolate chips

Pre-heat the oven to 100°C/200°F/Gas Mark Low

1 To make the biscuit crust, combine the crushed biscuits and the melted butter. Press into the bottom and on the sides of a 23cm/9in spring-form tin. Set aside.

2 Using an electric mixer, beat the cream cheese until smooth, then blend in the sugar. Add one egg at a time, beating well between additions. Add the cream, vanilla and instant coffee and beat well for 2 minutes, making sure the coffee is dissolved.

3 Pour the mixture into the prepared crust and sprinkle with the chocolate chips. Using a spatula, swirl the chocolate chips through the mixture. Place the tin on a baking tray and bake for about 2 hours, or until a cake tester inserted in the centre comes out clean. Allow to cool completely on a cooling rack before removing from the tin.

Serving suggestion: Chill this cheesecake thoroughly before serving.

Cherry Cream
Cheese Crown

Here's a really pretty dessert that is ideal to serve at teatime. I've suggested you use ready-prepared cherry pie filling bought in a tin, but of course when cherries are fresh, you can try making your own.

Serves 10
Preparation time: 35 minutes (plus overnight refrigeration)
Cooking time: 15 minutes

175g/6oz sponge fingers
50ml/2fl oz brandy
225g/8oz packet cream cheese, softened
75g/3oz sugar

450ml/16fl oz whipping cream
1 teaspoon vanilla essence
1 large tin cherry pie filling

1   Lightly grease the bottom of a 23cm/9in spring-form tin. Brush both sides of the sponge fingers with the brandy and line the sides of the tin with half the fingers, rounded sides facing out.

2   In a bowl beat the cream cheese using an electric mixer until smooth. Add the sugar gradually and continue to beat for 1 minute.

3   In another bowl, combine the cream and vanilla and beat until thick but not dry. Fold the cream into the cheese mixture and spread half in the bottom of the prepared tin. Arrange the remaining brandy fingers over the filling, rounded side up and top with the remaining filling. Cover and chill overnight.

4   Release the sides of the tin carefully and transfer the cake to a serving dish. Spread the cherry pie filling over the top, cover and refrigerate for at least 2 hours.

Serving suggestion: This cake should be served thoroughly chilled.

Little Stilton Tarts

**Makes 2
18cm/7in tarts
Preparation
time: 35
minutes (plus
refrigeration
time)
Cooking time:
20 minutes**

Here's a very easy, yet elegant, after-dinner cheese course.

*450g/1lb frozen puff
pastry, thawed
1 egg, beaten*

*150g/5oz Stilton cheese,
crumbled*

1   First roll out the pastry on a lightly-floured surface to a thickness of about 5mm/⅛in. Cut out two 18cm/7in rounds, then cut a 2cm/¾in rim off each round and put aside. Re-roll the rounds to 18cm/7in.

2   Place the rounds on a baking tray and brush the outer edge with the beaten egg. Position a cut pastry rim on top of each and refrigerate for at least 30 minutes.

Pre-heat the oven to 200°C/400°F/Gas Mark 6

3   Divide the cheese between the two tarts and brush the tart rims with more beaten egg. Be careful not to let the egg drip on the sides. Bake the tarts for about 20 minutes, or until golden-brown. Cool slightly on a cooling rack and serve warm.

Serving suggestion: Serve the tarts sliced like a pie.

Cheesey Crème Caramel

Here's a sweet cheese flan that really does resemble a crème caramel.

Serves 8
Preparation time: 30 minutes
Cooking time: 1½ hours

2 × 225g/8oz packets
cream cheese, softened
400g/14oz sugar
2 teaspoons vanilla essence

2 × 350g/12oz cans
evaporated milk
4 eggs

1   First, using a blender or food processor, blend together the cheese, half the sugar, eggs and vanilla until smooth.

Pre-heat the oven to 180°C/350°F/Gas Mark 4

2   Place the remaining sugar in a saucepan over a moderate heat until it caramelises. Watch it very carefully.

3   Pour the caramel into a soufflé dish and then pour the cheese mixture over the caramel. Set the dish in a deep pan and add enough simmering water to the pan to come half-way up the sides of the dish.

4   Bake for about 1½ hours, or until a cake tester inserted in the centre comes out clean. Allow to cool on a cooling rack, then invert on to a serving dish.

Serving suggestion: This dish can be served chilled or at room temperature.

Index